Zavod RAKMO

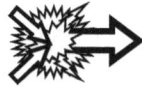

Communication Wellness

New Standards for Quality Communication in Organizations

Marko Iršič

Ljubljana, 2018

Communication Wellness
New Standards for Quality Communication in Organizations

Marko Iršič

Zavod RAKMO, Ljubljana, 2018
2nd edition

1.000 pieces
Price 24,90 €

Edited by Barbara Iršič
Cover design: NONPAREL d.o.o.
Layout: Serafin Storitve d.o.o.

info@rakmo.si

www.rakmo.si

First published in Ljubljana, Slovenija by Zavod RAKMO in 2017

CIP - Kataložni zapis o publikaciji
Narodna in univerzitetna knjižnica, Ljubljana

005.57

IRŠIČ, Marko
Communication wellness : new standards for quality
communication in organizations / Marko Iršič. - 2nd ed. –
Ljubljana : Zavod Rakmo, 2018

ISBN 978-961-92827-9-3

297964800

Praise for Communication Wellness

This is an extraordinary book, loaded with practical ideas and strategies to minimize conflict and improve communication in every area of business life.

Brian Tracy – Author – How the Best Leaders Lead

Communication Wellness builds on the transformative mediation framework and offers valuable insights about the crucial role of communication in conflict. Readers will find many helpful ideas about how to create and sustain constructive communication as difficult conflicts unfold.

Joseph P. Folger, Ph.D.,
Professor at Temple University, Philadelphia PA and current
president of the Institute for the Study of Conflict Transformation

Marko Iršič brings together a wealth of material from across the disciplines of mediation, workplace psychology, organisational change, and people development, in this comprehensive, practical and positive book that should enable any organisation to take effective steps to limit the damage that conflict causes to people and productivity.

Katherine Graham, Chair of CMP Resolutions and
Co-author of the book Mediation for Managers

Marko Iršič moves the paradigm of transformative mediation into a broader spectrum of communication, giving it a new sense of meaning and importance to society as a whole. He presents a practical and useful tool on how to gain more knowledge and awareness about constructive interaction, crucial to overall well-being in interpersonal communication. This will improve the transformative capacity of individuals, organizations and communities on how to deal with conflicts.

Reny Tuinstra, MfN-registered mediator and Coach,
Founder and Owner of Tuinstra Mediation

Marko Irsic takes the 'Promise of Mediation' to the next level, elaborating on how to address conflict before it escalates, for better interpersonal communication and improved relationships. A useful overview and concrete guide to humanizing our world."

Hania M. Fedorowicz,
European Institute for Community-based Conflict Resolution

The book addresses two fields -- transformative conflict theory and communications theory -- I read it with interest. I have no doubt that this book will be of great value -- I enjoyed it very much.

F. Peter Phillips, Business Conflict Management LLC,
Director of the Alternative Dispute Resolution Skills Program at New
York Law School

"Communication Wellness" does a great job of looking at new approaches to understanding, examining, managing, and mending productive and constructive communication. This book is unique since it views communication and conflict through the transformative framework lens. Employers and employees alike will benefit from reading this book.

Michelle Zaremba, Director of Dayton Mediation Center,
Fellow of Institute for the Study of Conflict Transformation, Author
of The Wheels on Fire

Conflicts are a part of our daily lives. It sounds absurd, but conflicts offer great opportunities to develop our mutual relationships. For that purpose, they need to be detected and resolved at their earliest stage. Quality communication can be of great help in that. This book offers many useful tips for developing communication skills and invites us to progress in communication, even when there is no conflict yet. Communication wellness is proposed as a useful approach to development of the potential for early resolution of situations that can lead to conflict.

Stanislav Lenart, PhD, Assistant Professor at University of
Ljubljana, Former Chief Scout of the Slovenian Catholic Girl Guides
and Boy Scouts Association

Often conflict is only thought about after it becomes negative and destructive, but this book looks at ways to think about conflict at every phase, even before it starts. Marko Iršič explores innovative approach for building "communication wellness," including practical strategies for addressing communication challenges proactively.

Janet Mueller, Mediator, Mediation Trainer, Fellow of the Institute for the study of Conflict Transformation

Conflicts occur also in professional sports. Precisely for that reason it is of utmost importance that athletes deal with their dilemmas or doubts with quality communication as soon as possible. Consequently, they have the best chances for progress and top results. Communication wellness is the right recipe for long-term success in any field. Therefore, I am very happy that we received this book that will help many, including athletes and their teams in professional sports.

Natalija Gros, former professional sports climber, World Cup combined overall winner 2007 and European Champion 2008

Marko Iršič's book is a wonderful description of the transformative process and an exploration into how we can address conflict in a more timely and efficient manner. Nothing could be better than to find a way to communicate in a healthy way. Finding a way to communicate well and create space for constructive conflict to lead us to positive insights is a great goal to strive for. I highly recommend this book for anyone who would like to find ways to address conflict and transform negative interactions to positive interactions!

Lisa Singh, Coach, Trainer, Facilitator and Mediator

I like the term »Communication Wellness«. I have learned a lot about the nature of conflict and how to avoid and resolve them. We all need to know more about what communication wellness is and how to be better in communication. Unfortunately, we learn many less useful things in school but almost nothing about communication. I recommend this book to everyone – from experts to people that like to read and learn useful new things!

Aleš Lisac, Author, Lecturer, Marketing Advisor and Expert in Direct Marketing

I work with many different companies and I see that recognising and managing conflicts appropriately presents a crucial element of the success of a company. The book Communication Wellness is an excellent tool for all who are leading others!

Saša Einsiedler,
Communication Skills Trainer, Coach and Author

Anyone is concerned with physical wellness. More and more people are concerned with mental/spiritual wellness. But very few people even imagine that communication wellness could exist.

Marko Iršič's book brilliantly demonstrates that communication wellness is not only desirable but also that it is possible. Moreover, Marko Iršič shows that it can be fairly easily achieved in organizations and, why not, in your family.

Some large organizations such as the World Bank and the United Nations are promoting such programs for their staff and managers. I can witness that Marko Iršič is not a dreamer. When such programs are put in place, they work incredibly well, and "wellness" becomes an accurate word to describe the relations between members of the organization.

Thierry Garby,
Mediator, Founder of UIA World Forum of Mediation Centers,
Author of Agreed! Negotiation and Mediation in the 21st century

I have known Marko Iršič for many years through our work with the World Forum of Mediation Centers. From the outset, he has been immersed in the training, practice and spread of transformative mediation. I applaud Marko for writing this book and his goals for doing so. If transformative mediation can get a foothold in the workplace, it will introduce countless individuals to the process and its benefits and could be an excellent springboard for the use of this important dispute resolution technology throughout all aspects of human relations.

Jeffry S. Abrams, Mediator, Arbitrator, Former President of
Association of Attorney-Mediators, Member of advisory board of UIA
World Forum of Mediation Centers

Table of Contents

Introduction

It is well observed and documented that negative conflict has detrimental effects on relationships, psychological and physiological health, quality of performance, motivation and efficiency, as well as wellbeing in general.

Despite this general recognition of the impact of conflict, we as a human race have neither developed a knowledge base nor culture to successfully manage conflict. The most common responses to conflict are ending communication and ignoring conflict or even violence, which in turn only makes conflict worse. On top of that, the common perception of the source of conflict is that it is the other person's fault; that he or she is mean, crazy, egotistical, etc.

Indications of that are court disputes, divorces, wars, violence, bad relationships, workplace dissatisfaction, psychological and psychosomatic illnesses, to mention just a few.

However, there exist many inspiring stories of successful relationships, companies, organizations and groups that manage conflicts well and, even more, demonstrate a high quality of communication most of the time. And it is not just luck. Knowingly or intuitively they are doing some things differently.

In the last decades mediation as a tool for amicable conflict resolution emerged and it is commonly used in some countries, especially in court disputes. However, mediation most commonly focuses primarily on settlement and is used very late in the conflict span. Therefore, although it is a magnificent tool it does not contribute to the wellbeing of people and society as much as it could since it is not used enough and starts normally very late in the process.

Even less than knowledge of how to deal with conflict, have people developed the knowledge base and culture for communication wellness and standards for quality communication. There are many programs, books, training courses, etc., dealing with these issues, but neither organizations nor society in general have adopted the culture of communication wellness.

This does not mean that human beings in general do not appreciate the experience of high-quality communication, but we do not have appropriate tools nor understanding of communication dynamics nor general awareness or standards of a high level of communication nor mechanisms for its reparation when it deteriorates.

This book proposes a new approach to perceiving, assessing, managing and repairing the quality of communication and offers some practical tools.

Chapter one illustrates and proposes a general overview of communication and conflict dynamics through the transformative perspective, briefly discusses characteristics of destructive, as well as constructive conflict interaction and elaborates on key concepts of empowerment and recognition. Then the notion of transformative communication is explored and an overview of basic transformative communication skills is presented.

Chapter two discusses mediation as a useful tool to manage conflicts in an organization or a community and proposes different types of mediation in relation to stages of conflict. Furthermore, it discusses the model of implementing in-house mediation and points out the shortcomings of relying only on mediation and suggests that, in addition to mediation, a more general system and commitment is needed to effectively manage and prevent conflict, as well as maintain a high quality of communication in an organization or a community.

Chapter three elaborates on stages of conflict based on two different models: Glasl's nine-stage model of conflict escalation and the six-stage model of conflict transformation. Additionally, three levels of conflict management in relation to consequences of conflict are discussed.

Chapter four describes the characteristics of conflict resilient organizations and presents the concept of conflict competence as a trait of individuals who tend to handle conflicts well. It also proposes a tool for assessment of conflict competence by individual members of the organization. It shows a link between the level of conflict competence and the general quality of communication. It then describes in detail the notion of the conflict/communication spiral and proposes a mapping perspective in interpersonal communication including communication pitfalls.

Chapter five illustrates the consequences of late conflict intervention or lack thereof and also discusses the reasons why people tend to avoid conflict. It underlines the importance of an early-stage conflict intervention, as well as the development of the capacity for personal strength and responsiveness, and the development of quality communication as a norm in an organization.

Chapter six describes the concept of communication wellness in detail and makes a distinction between a general state of affairs and an intervention. It also describes the use of a tool (questionnaire) for assessing the level of communication wellness in the organization, namely, for a particular situation, for a particular relationship in general and for a group or organization in general.

Chapter seven touches on and discusses various options for intervention and suggests criteria for their use or implementation. In particular, it draws attention to communication first aid and the notion of mandatory mediation as the 'work assignment' or 'professional responsibility' of the employee or manager, as well as referral to mediation when disruption of communication wellness is noticed.

Chapter eight proposes and describes new communication standards for companies and organizations, and suggests options for their implementation.

1. The Transformative View of Conflict and Communication

This chapter illustrates and proposes a general overview of communication and conflict dynamics through the transformative perspective, briefly discusses the characteristics of destructive, as well as constructive conflict interaction and elaborates on key concepts of empowerment and recognition. Then the notion of transformative communication is explained and explored and an overview of basic transformative communication skills is presented.

The transformative view of conflict, briefly presented below, was well explained in the work of Robert A. Baruch Bush and Joseph P. Folger (1994, 2005), where a transformative model of mediation was articulated. However, the model of communication presented in their work is obviously broader and transcends mediation and even conflict, for that matter. It is useful for observing and analyzing any communication or interaction in general.

The Transformative View of Conflict

In a destructive conflict people experience relative weakness and self-absorption. In conflict, we often feel unsettled, confused, fearful, disorganized, unsure, anxious, etc. (state of weakness) and also self-protective, defensive, suspicious, focused on our own interests, thoughts and feelings (self-absorption). If both parties feel that way, their interaction will almost invariably be destructive, which will in turn only contribute to their state of relative weakness and self-absorption within that interaction or that relationship.

Conflict is a crisis of human interaction. It tends to destabilize parties' experience of self and the other. People in conflict tend to experience relative weakness and self-absorption. These negative dynamics tend to feed into each other in a vicious circle. As a result, the interaction quickly degenerates and assumes a mutually destructive, alienating and dehumanizing character (Bush and Folger, 2005).

However, despite the destabilizing impact of conflict, people have the ability to rebound and recover from its alienating effects. Specifically, people can and indeed do make dynamic shifts along two dimensions while conflict unfolds: empowerment (shifts towards increasing clarity, confidence, personal strength, organization, decisiveness) and recognition (shifts towards increasing attentiveness to the other, responsiveness to the other, openness to the other's humanity and appreciation for the other's situation). Thus, despite the potentially destructive impacts of conflict, people have the capacity to move back into their sense of personal strength or self-confidence (the empowerment shift) and into their sense of openness or responsiveness to the other (the recognition shift). As these positive shifts feed into each other, the interaction can regenerate and assume a constructive, connecting, and humanizing character (Bush and Folger, 2005).

If people are interacting constructively, they often feel calmer, clearer, more confident, more focused, more decisive, more articulate, etc. (state of strength) and they are also more attentive to the other, more open, more able to see the other's perspective, willing to consider the other's interests and their feelings (responsiveness). If people are interacting in a state of strength and responsiveness to the other, the outcome of their interaction will most likely be constructive and will bring even more clarity and strength, as well as more willingness to be responsive to the other.

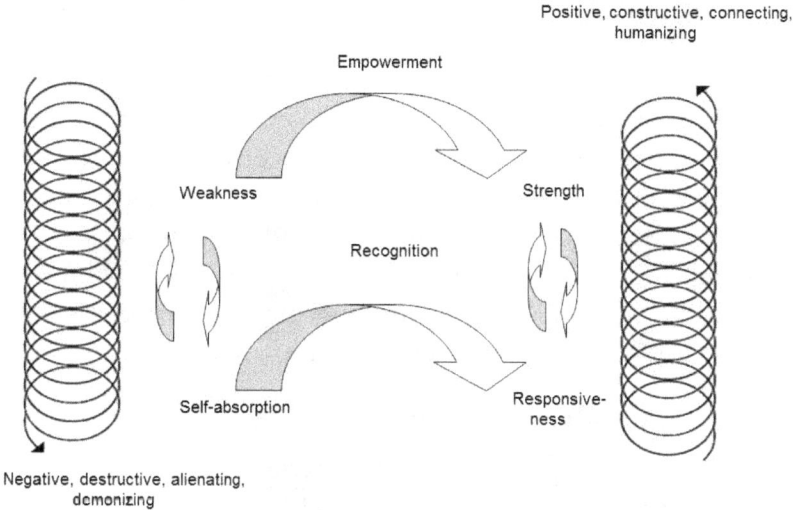

Figure 1: Model of conflict transformation (Bush and Folger, 2005)

But what happens if one party is in a state of strength and responsiveness and the other in a state of weakness and self-absorption? That is an unstable combination which does not last long, and it can go either way, depending on the intensity or stability of the one or the other. Oftentimes, the one who is in a state of weakness and self-absorption to a certain extent 'surprises' the other who is maybe in a normal mode of strength and responsiveness, and consequently drags him or her down to a state of weakness and self-absorption. On the other hand, if the other party is either prepared or strong enough, he or she can gradually contribute to the first party regaining strength and responsiveness.

Destructive and Constructive Conflict Interaction

Conflicts are a fact of life, how we respond to them, however, determines their outcome. If when confronted with conflict we interact constructively, there will most likely be a constructive outcome. On the other hand, if we interact in a destructive manner, the outcome will most certainly not be what we would like. The problem is, however, that we oftentimes do not notice the destructiveness of interaction until it is too late, or even if we notice it, we are often not able to change it. Nobody consciously decides they will engage in destructive interaction and, on top of that, interaction is already by definition something that transcends an individual. So how can we improve our interaction if it is not only up to us. Before we focus on that question, let us first explore the characteristics of destructive and those of constructive conflict interaction.

Destructive Conflict Interaction

Using a metaphor, we can describe destructive conflict interaction as a vicious circle which nobody likes but does not know how to exit either and is in most cases contributing to its persistence. Destructive conflict interaction is characterized by negative actions, destructive behavior, alienation and demonizing the other.

What is also characteristic of destructive conflict interaction is seeing the whole thing as the other person's fault, accusing or attacking, not being willing or able to listen to the other, not willing to consider the validity of the other's point of view, trying to prove them wrong, explaining the same things repeatedly, giving more examples of the same point to prove its validity, being stuck or rigid in statements and demands, focusing on positions rather than on needs or common ground.

In addition, negative emotions are increasingly present (being upset, angry, hurt, frustrated, afraid, tense, etc.) and as a consequence, verbal and nonverbal communication is becoming more and more tense. There can even be passive aggression, threats of leaving or even ending the relationship and eventually the communication is ended unilaterally by one of the parties. In the worst cases, there can also be violence and abuse.

A strong element of destructive conflict interaction is also perceiving and treating the other as bad or evil, which has the characteristics of a 'self-fulfilling prophecy' since by acting towards the others as if they were evil, we force them to react destructively in defense, which we only see as proof that we were right about them in the first place.

Constructive Conflict Interaction

Constructive conflict interaction, on the other hand, is characterized by being more and more productive. It contributes to the parties feeling progressively clearer and more understood, confident and responsive, calm and creative.

It is characterized by movement, flexibility, positive emotion (excitement, relief, insight, being understood, etc.) and focusing on the main message, listening to the other party and responding favorably to what they are saying, trying to understand and repeating what they have said, acknowledging them and showing appreciation, accepting responsibility and searching for options that would accommodate both sides.

As a consequence, communication is becoming progressively calmer and rewarding, giving insights and ideas, giving the sense of collaboration and common effort and satisfaction with progress made, and new clarity and understanding gained. There are also expressions of appreciation given to the other and possibly apologies for one's own behavior and wrong assumptions about the other.

Combination of Both

In reality it is often a combination of both types of interaction, so it is tricky to establish what is going on and it can change from one moment to another. Or when things seem to be going well, they suddenly change without any apparent reason.

The key, however, is not where the interaction starts but in which direction it goes? i.e. Is the interaction becoming progressively destructive or is it becoming more and more constructive. The interaction will most likely start at or quickly drop to the level of quality where it was left the previously. Therefore, the key question is how to support the elements that are characteristic of constructive interaction and how to diffuse or transform the elements that are characteristic of destructive interaction. It turns out that both can be achieved by focusing on empowerment and recognition shifts in a specific interaction.

Empowerment and Recognition

Since empowerment and recognition shifts are the crucial elements of conflict transformation or communication becoming progressively more constructive, let us explore these concepts a little bit further.

Empowerment

Empowerment means a shift towards increasing clarity, confidence, personal strength, organization and decisiveness, and it can be related among others to goals, options, resources, skills and decision-making (Bush and Folger, 1994).

In terms of goals, empowerment means that it becomes more clear to the party what are his/her goals, needs and interests and that they are important and deserve consideration.

In terms of options, empowerment means that the parties are more aware of the range of options available to them, as well as their control over those options; that they have choices about how to handle the issue and whether to stay or leave a particular situation and that regardless of the external constraints they have at least some choices available to them.

In terms of resources, empowerment means becoming aware of resources the party already possesses (including having something that is valuable to the other party) and becoming aware of possible resources which could be available to them or becoming aware that resources available could suffice to reach an outcome previously not considered.

In terms of skills, empowerment refers to the development or increased use of conflict resolution or communication skills, including the ability to listen, express oneself, organize and analyze issues, present arguments, brainstorm and evaluate alternative solutions.

In terms of decision-making, empowerment refers to conscious deliberation, consideration and making decisions while taking into account the possible impact or consequences of such decisions (including what to do in terms of settling the dispute, how to settle it, and whether or not to settle it at all) and a clear realization that decisions are in their hands and up to them.

Recognition

Recognition shifts are shifts towards increasing attentiveness to the other, responsiveness to the other, openness to the other's humanity and appreciation for the other's situation. Recognition can be observed in terms of capacity to give recognition, desire for giving recognition, giving recognition in thought, giving recognition in words and giving recognition in action (Bush and Folger, 1994).

The capacity to give recognition means the sense of inner strength and stability which is big enough to allow us to be able to consider the other person's perspective as opposed to a state of disempowerment which disables us from focusing on anything else but ourselves (our pain, our needs, our fear etc.)

19

The desire for giving recognition is a further step in terms of recognition and it means that besides being able to, we also want to consider or try to understand the other person's perspective.

Giving recognition in thought means that we do not only try to but we successfully gain insights in to the other party's perspective (intentions, motivation, difficulty, etc.) and as a consequence perceive them less malevolent and treat them with greater consideration than before.

Giving recognition in words means verbally expressing appreciation of the other party's situation or expressing different, more favorable understanding of the other party's conduct.

Giving recognition in action refers to proposing solutions or accepting agreement that accommodates, at least to some extent, the other party's needs or situation, or changing one's own behavior as a response to new insights or understanding of the other's situation or desires.

Empowerment in general precedes recognition. When people are in the state of weakness they also tend to be self-absorbed and consequently less able to be responsive. The stronger and calmer they are, the more they are able to be responsive to others. Recognition shifts are therefore occurring more often later in the transformative process. At the same time, recognition given from one party has a strong empowering effect on the other, which in turn makes them more able to give recognition back.

What do People Want When They are in Conflict?

To use the words of one of our participants in a training course for mediators: "When I am in conflict, I feel bad and I want to get out of it!". That captures the idea of conflict transformation in a nutshell.

People in general want out of the conflict. And there are at least five ways to do so:

1. to end the relationship or leave the environment (escape);
2. to subordinate the other(s);
3. to give in/conform to the other(s);
4. to abandon the issue; or
5. to transform interaction.

In general, people are very well prepared to use the first four, but much less so to use the fifth, which is, especially if things are important to us, the most rewarding but also the most difficult. In addition, it is not common practice and many people have neither knowledge nor skills to use it.

The first four all take their toll. Obviously, we lose the relationship in the first one, in the second one we become a sort of a tyrant and cannot really trust the others since they are likely to challenge our domination, if we give in in the third, we lose what we want or need and if we abandon the issue in the fourth, things do not get resolved. Of course, if things are not important, abandoning the issue (either by humor, changing the topics, explicit invitation to drop the issue etc.) or giving in if things are not important to us but are important to the other is quite appropriate, but things are different when the issue is important to both.

People in general want to get out of conflict quickly and unfortunately they often use the way which might seem easier or more appropriate at the moment but brings undesired consequences in the long run.

The first four strategies are in fact not resolving the issue as such but are in a way avoiding conflict. Only the fifth option leads through conflict and the parties can benefit from the opportunities for growth which the conflict brings. It is however usually the most difficult since it requires internal strength and openness to the other's point of view, which are two qualities that are extremely rare in conflict. This is also why it is severely underused. Interaction can be transformed using transformative communication which is briefly discussed below.

Transformative Communication

Transformative communication is the form of communication which has the potential of transforming interaction for the better. And has the potential to improve quality of interaction and, consequently, the relationship between communicating parties. But in any case, it has the potential of transforming a situation and helping the parties to better understand themselves and each other and to work together, to cooperate, to solve problems, to clarify misunderstandings or achieve their goals.

The term transformative communication describes a specific form of communication. It does not refer to the exchange of information or the everyday common communication. It refers specifically to a high-quality communication between parties either in terms of resolving a certain conflict or issue or in terms of improving their relationship, quality of interaction or communication with each other, or working on certain issues or problems that they want to solve – which does not necessarily mean that there is a conflict or discrepancy between them. It can also be used for creative problem solving.

In general, it refers to the communication between parties which has the effect of improving the quality of either their relationship, their communication or their cooperation, or enhances their collaboration or problem solving.

It refers also to supporting one party when he or she experiences a dilemma, conflict or problem, either within himself or with somebody else or with more people. In that case, transformative communication supports the speaking party in working through his/her dilemma, conflict or problem.

Transformative communication in a broader sense refers also to communication or cooperation which involves the use of elements of transformative communication or transformative communication skills even if it is not all the time aiming at transformation or improving the quality of interaction between the parties or offering transformative support to the speaking party.

In the narrower sense, however, transformative communication refers to 1.) supporting one party with his/her dilemmas, conflicts or problems or 2.) supporting two or more parties in communication between them or 3.) using the skills of transformative communication by the parties themselves when trying to resolve certain problems or issues or trying to improve the quality of their interaction.

In the transformative mode of communication, transformative communication skills are used.

Transformative Communication Skills

If people are communicating in a state of strength and responsiveness, their conversation will most likely be productive and fulfilling. If a situation is difficult, however, there is a danger that communication will become difficult and even destructive, which will not benefit either side.

In order to prevent destructive communication, or to contribute to it being even more productive, we can use some relatively simple skills which, however, become increasingly less available to the parties when conflict escalates. In such a case the support of a trained mediator who is not involved in the conflict is helpful.

The skills will be described in general without differentiating who is using them: a mediator, a non-formal mediator or a party. A word of caution is, however, in order. Namely even if transformative communication skills seem easy this is not the case, especially in a conflict situation, and cannot be adequately learned or fully appreciated by only reading this book (or any book for that matter) or the description in this chapter. They should be practiced, observed and experienced in a communication situation or in training. By describing them in this book, we merely want to illustrate and point out the skills and their impact, as well as some key aspects of using them, and it is not meant that the reader would learn sufficiently by reading about them.

The most basic of transformative communication skills is **reflection**. By reflection we mean repeating back to the speaker the main points he or she expressed verbally or nonverbally, including links and possible inconsistencies among them. To be effective reflection should be done without judgement. It is not enough that we do not express our judgement or opinion, it has to be that we set it aside for the time being and we try to grasp the situation from the speakers point of view.

In *reflecting* a party statement, the mediator simply says what he hears the party saying, using words close to the party's own language, even (or especially) when the language is strong, loud, negative or strongly expressive. The mediator does not soften the party's language or remove its "sting" (Folger & Bush, 2010, pp. 39).

The act of reflecting to the speaker has a strong empowering effect. It helps the speaker to clarify, elaborate, amend or change what he or she is saying. Reflection also gives the speaker a feeling that they are heard and understood.

Reflection can be used in different ways. It can be for example short or long, partial or holistic, superficial or deep, etc., sometimes only a word or a phrase is the best reflection. At other times, much longer and elaborate reflection is appropriate. Similarly, sometimes a detail of conversation has to be supported and at other times a more comprehensive description of one's situation or position is in order.

For reflection to be effective it is important that a person is focused and does not think about other things when doing it but tries to follow the message of the other side as closely as possible. If it is done absentmindedly, it can also have the opposite effect. At the same time, it has to be focused on the main parts of the message of the speaker, otherwise it can easily cause more confusion than clarity. And it is the most useful when emotions or ambiguities are high or when the subject matter is complex or confusing. If we were to use reflection when the other is communicating clearly and calmly or if it is focused on nonessential parts of the message, it can be annoying and it can have a disruptive effect on the conversation.

Mediators are trained and must be skilled in using reflection in a way that follows the speaker's message without adding or changing something. Ordinary people, however, if not trained to do it the right way, even when trying to use it, are quick to interpret words in their own way and to add things that were not said nor meant by the speaker. It is important to do it right if it is to be effective.

It helps if we mentally separate what the other person is saying from what we are thinking or believing to be true. If the other party is saying something, even if we repeat it, it does not mean that we agree with it, nor does it mean it is the truth. If we use such a mental stance, it makes it much easier to use reflection the right way, that is following what the speaker is really expressing. Additionally, using reflection helps us distance ourselves from the message of the speaker and preserve our own perspective unthreatened.

Summarizing as a skill refers to capturing and organizing the conversation (or part of it) between the parties, which includes topics and points of view of all the parties (it can be done by a neutral third party or by one of the participants). Like reflection, summary should also be done without judgement or bias. Summary merely states what was said and includes both or all participants.

Once the parties start talking directly with each other, *summary* may be the preferred response, rather than reflection. ... In a summary, the mediator *speaks to and with both parties* and includes larger blocks, or "chunks", of the party conversation or interaction (Folger & Bush, 2010, pp. 41).

Summary includes naming the theme (e.g. working hours) and the position of each individual (e.g. one thinks they should be fixed and the other that they should be flexible). Summary should include the themes where parties disagree, together with their respective points of view but should also include points of agreement or common ground. Interestingly enough, the parties in conflict often do not even notice similarities and agreements since they are focused so much on 'getting one's own message across'.

Summary can be done in relation to a smaller part of the conversation or can try to capture the conversation as a whole. It can refer to more superficial aspects of conversation (e.g. facts or details) or it can reach deep (e.g. values or attitudes). And it can point out differences or similarities between the parties.

Summary has a substantial empowering effect. The parties do not only understand their respective positions better but they also get a better understanding of the bigger scheme of the conversation and by that they gain better control over conversation, which increases their strength.

Summary also has a strong potential for the recognition shift. In addition to seeing the field of their conversation more clearly, the parties can also place the perspective of the other person in the context and by that they are already abandoning the black and white attitude and maybe changing the perception of the other's opinion from wrong to different.

Summary is most effective when both parties are already relatively empowered. If it is used too soon in conflict interaction, it can even have the opposite effect since the parties that are in the state of weakness tend to perceive it as imposing the other person's perspective. If they are already empowered enough, then summary can help them make the recognition shift in terms of better understanding the other and maybe even seeing him in a more favorable light than before.

Checking in as a skill refers to asking questions that point out decision points in the conversation or interaction. Questions which can also be implicit (e.g. just listing several options mentioned up to that moment) are related to and stemming from current conversation or interaction, they point out decision points and leave or give back the responsibility for decisions to the parties.

"Checking in", however, is an important and effective addition to the other essential skills and is frequently coupled with reflection or summary. … It is often used as intervention when it seems that parties have come to a choice point in mediation, and it provides them with opportunity to make clear decisions (Folger & Bush, 2010, pp. 43).

Questions should be sincere and not suggestive or leading. They should merely point out the decision points and leave the decision to the parties. If checking in is used by one of the parties themselves, they can subsequently propose their view on the decision, ask the other party what they think about it or even just wait for the other party to respond. If checking in is used by the mediator, they should just wait for the response of the parties or if there is none, continue with other interventions without insisting that the parties respond to the question.

In each communication and interaction, including conflict, there are many decisions we make automatically even without realizing it. If interaction is productive, that is all fine and well. However, when our choices and responses contribute to destructive interaction, it is helpful if some light is shed on decision points in order to make it possible to make conscious decisions (which would more likely contribute to constructive development) rather than automatic decisions (which would contribute to destructive interaction).

Checking in, if used appropriately, can be a very powerful technique and can shift the process most rapidly for the better. At the same time, it is also the most dangerous since there is the most potential that the one who is asking questions would (even without realizing) indirectly direct conversation or suggest the outcome of a decision point, which would have the opposite effect.

Getting Out or Staying Out

The fourth skill is knowing when to be silent and just listen, which is especially important for a mediator but also for using in our own communication. In terms of mediation it means that a mediator consciously refrains or withdraws from interaction and remains silent in order to make it possible for the parties to talk directly to each other without interrupting them, or to think about things that they have heard or about new aspects they became aware of or to communicate with each other at the nonverbal level.

Silence can be an intentional response by the mediator in at least two different situations. First, when parties are directly engaging, the mediator's silently "backing out" and nonintervention can support party decision-making and communication. Second, during and after a period of intense conversation, "staying out" to allow time both for the exchange and for some reflection after the exchange, is also an appropriate mediator response (Folger & Bush, 2010, pp. 44).

Also in our own communication, this skill is appropriate in terms of letting the other party think about what we have said or about what they are processing, or check in with themselves their various options, etc. or when there is important nonverbal communication going on.

Comparing the Skills

In terms of focus and the outcome of using specific skills we could suggest that reflection is focused on the individual (point of view, situation, emotions and feelings, etc.) and aims at a greater understanding of the individual (by themselves and by the other party). Summarizing is focused on the conversation (contents and topics) and aims at making the conversation as a whole (issues that were brought up, where the parties agree or disagree, how the issues are related to each other, etc.) more clear to all parties; and checking in is related to the process (the way parties interact and how to continue, as well as which attitude or understanding to adopt) and aims at making decision points more salient to the parties and thus contributing to the parties making conscious rather than automatic decisions.

Skill	Reflection	Summarizing	Checking-in
Focus	**Individual** (point of view, situation and experience)	**Conversation** (topics and contents)	**Process** (procedure and mode of communication)
Outcome	Understanding of individual (facts and feelings)	Understanding conversation (topics and contents) **and the other**	Understanding of choices (decisions and attitudes)

Table 1: Comparing transformative communication skills

On the pages above, when presenting the skills, they are presented regardless of whether they are used by the mediator or by (one of) the parties. Obviously, there are some important differences in the use and manifestation of skills, if they are used by a neutral third party or by one or both (all) of the parties. It goes beyond the scope of this book to describe in detail the differences or to even describe in detail practical use of the skills in either context (as mediator or as a party). As already pointed out, the skills should be learned in practice (e.g. in a training course) and practiced in order to fully appreciate their use and to gain experience and ability to use them skillfully.

Priorities of Issues

In general, issues are linked to each other and therefore interwoven. Consequently, it sometimes does not make sense to discuss one issue at a time. However, there are orders of priorities that are wise to follow. In general, when talking to each other, people most of the time do not consciously distinguish among these orders of priorities and are primarily focused on the content of the conversation.

However, there are two aspects of communication that have a stronger impact on interaction than the subject matter, namely feelings, emotions and relationship issues and even more so the way people are talking or interacting (The process aspect of interaction).

It is the way how people are interacting that has the strongest impact on the immediate interaction. For example, if people are shouting or insulting each other on the one hand or talking calmly on the other, if they are taking turns in listening and speaking or interrupting each other, if they are focusing on one issue at a time or they are jumping from topic, to topic, etc. What also plays a role is the general characteristic of interaction between the parties or what they believe that the characteristic is, e.g. *He talks aggressively! She never says what she thinks! He is interrupting me and does not listen! She is so emotional!*, etc.

The second strongest impact is the level of emotion, feelings and relationship. If we are angry, for example, it has an impact on our behavior, on our thinking and on our decision-making capacity. People tend to make different decisions when they are angry than when they are calm. If we feel depressed, this again has an impact on our thinking and also on our perception and interpretation. People tend to interpret the same situations and behavior differently when they feel down in comparison to when they feel happy. Feelings of anger, sadness, frustration, disappointment, fear, worry and so on have a real impact on interaction and also on decision making of the parties and obviously on the capacity to listen to each other. Luckily, it is often a huge help if the feelings are heard and understood, by a third party but even more so by the other side. It does not make sense to disagree about feelings in terms you should not feel this way or your feelings are wrong (e.g. don't be sad, calm down, you are always in a bad mood, etc.). Although there is some sense in such remarks or attitudes, that normally does not help. It is much more useful to name the feeling we are noticing (e.g. you are angry) or ask: 'How do you feel?'.

And only the third in terms of impact and priority is the subject matter, practical issues or contents of communication. The irony is, however, that communication most of the time starts with practical aspects and it seems that this is the point of conflict. This is also one of the reasons why settlement driven or problem solving mediation is much different than transformative mediation. This does not mean that practical aspects and facts are not important but the fact is that the reason why conflict is so difficult most of the time does not lie in facts or practical aspects (although this is also sometimes the case) but in attitudes, feelings, emotions and relationship. For example, in a good relationship the same situation may not be a problem at all whereas in a bad relationship it may present an unsolvable problem. In addition, when we are calm and rational the same facts appear different than when we are, for example, angry.

Priority	Aspect of communication	Examples
3	Facts and ideas	I think ... I propose... I paid... I want my money back... It would be best if...
2	Feelings, emotions and relationship	sadness, fear, anger, disappointment: you don't care, you think only about yourself, you always...
1	Process	Don't shout!; You interrupted me! or Let me finish; I don't want you to call me that!; You don't listen!

Table 2: Aspects of communication and their priorities

Intrapersonal Transformative Communication Skills

In addition to the skills described above which are more of an interactive nature (e.g. how we speak and when we refrain from speaking), there are a few skills which are possibly even more important and are more intrapersonal in nature.

Assessing One's Own Internal Strength

Assessing or being aware of our own internal state (weakness or strength) plays a major role in how productive communication is going to be, since when we are interacting in the state of weakness it is more likely that the interaction is going to be destructive, especially if the other party is in a state of weakness as well. Whenever we are angry, upset, hurt or feel frustrated or are rigid in our position or when we want to 'impose' our message, perception or beliefs to the other, there is a good chance that we are in a state of weakness and that will negatively impact the interaction. On the other hand, when we feel calm, focused, clear and are willing and able to listen and try to understand the other, there is a good chance that the interaction is going to be productive or that we are going to contribute to it being such.

Distancing Oneself from the Speaker's Statement

Being able to distance oneself from what the other is saying is a very important skill. It, by itself, significantly increases our state of strength. If we are not able to leave the responsibility for words and actions to the other and perceive them as manifestations of their situation (although there is obviously some interaction as well), then we are inevitably in the role of a victim.

For example, if somebody says (to us) something bad about us or even insulting, it is a common reaction to feel hurt or upset. However, it does not make sense. Why should we be upset if the other is delusional or wrong? On the other hand, if he is right, by being hurt we could prevent ourselves from processing it and making a change for the better. And if the other says something that is correct, but in a

33

way which is disrespectful or insulting, why should we be hurt or upset if the other person is impolite?

It does not mean, however, that anything is acceptable or that we should tolerate certain behavior just because we are not hurt. On the contrary, if we are not hurt, we can set the boundaries or give the other person feedback even more efficiently than otherwise. And at the same time, we can offer more support to the other since being impolite, upset or insulting is in most cases a sign of an internal state of weakness.

If the other person is saying something we disagree with or which contradicts our values, it does not mean that we agree if we try to understand and do not get upset about it. On the contrary, it increases the chances that the other person will be able to listen and maybe modify their point of view.

The skill of distancing oneself psychologically from what the other person is saying is crucial for mediators to remain neutral. Namely, if they are not able to do so, they would get involved in the subject matter and would not be able to adequately support the conversation of the parties.

This is also very important for our own conversations. If the other party is saying something that we do not agree with, it does not mean it is true and there is no need for us to get upset or try to force the other side to change his or her statement. Even more, he or she may be saying something bad about us which is not true (at least in our mind) but it is their statement (not the truth) which is also connected to their internal state (e.g. weakness), so why should we be upset?

At first glance, it may seem unnatural or 'cold'. We are humans and it is only natural to respond by being upset or hurt if the other behaves in a certain way. However, if that were true, everybody would respond the same way in a similar situation, which is certainly not the case. The next counter argument could be: we respond or react differently because we have different patterns. So if we have different patterns, then we can also learn new ones.

To make a long story short, if we do not like how we respond to a certain situation automatically, we can learn a different response and therefore it is obvious that words or behavior of the other (even if it may trigger them) do not cause our response. It is up to us (even if we do not know it) how we are going to respond and feel.

Therefore, with some training and practice it is very possible to learn to distance oneself psychologically from the other's words, positions and behavior.

Regaining Internal Stability

Closely related to the previous skill is regaining internal stability. If we notice we are in a state of weakness, it is important to be able to regain internal strength if we want interaction to be productive. If we feel angry, for example, we can ask ourselves: *Do I want to feel angry? How do I want to feel? How do I want to respond?*, or we can say to ourselves: *Why should I feel angry if he/she is doing (or saying) this or that.* As soon as we notice how we feel, we can consciously choose how we want to feel (e.g. calm) and how we want to respond. It is simply by asking ourselves this question that we can drastically improve our sense of strength.

If we are, for example, in the role of a mediator and we are getting angry, there is a good chance that we are not doing our job. Maybe we lost our neutrality? Or maybe we are angry because a party is repeating the same things again and again, because we are not trying to listen and understand and not reflecting well enough and, therefore, the party does not feel heard nor understood. In such cases, regaining internal stability is relatively simple. Just increase the effort to listen and understand and obviously to reflect what the party was saying.

Assessing the Internal State of Strength of the Other

Assessing the internal state of the other is also important since it has a tendency to impact our sense of strength. We can assess how the other person feels based on how his or her behavior makes us feel (or to be more precise, which feelings or emotions it triggers in us), especially if we did not feel like that before. Based on the assessment of the internal state of the other, we can choose our response accordingly.

For example, if the other is in a state of weakness, it does not make sense to try to explain something to him or her since there is a slim chance that it would work. In such a case, we can either decide to try to listen and understand (empathically) while remaining calm or if we also feel or are starting to feel weak, propose to postpone the conversation (possibly also by explaining that we too feel upset) or engage in transformative support to help interaction remain constructive. Namely, if both parties are upset and try to explain something to the other, it is most likely (unless one or both change their internal state) that nobody will be able to listen and consequently nobody will feel heard and interaction will most likely deteriorate, making the problem even worse than it was in the first place.

Assessing the Quality of Interaction

It is also crucial to be able to, at least to a certain degree, correctly assess constructiveness of interaction. If the conversation gets stuck or is escalating in terms of becoming more violent, those are clear signs that the conversation is not being productive. But there are more subtle signs as well.

If the conversation is loud, it does not mean it is not constructive and if the conversation seems polite and calm, it does not mean it is constructive. Incorrectly assessing the constructiveness of interaction or not being aware if it can contribute to us responding (either in the role of a mediator or a party) the wrong way.

For example, if the mediator fails to correctly asses, that the interaction is becoming more destructive and consequently fails to intervene, things are likely to get worse.

Also in our everyday or work-related situations if, when speaking to someone, we fail to recognize that interaction is becoming destructive and thereby fail to respond appropriately, one or both parties will sooner or later not be able to tolerate it any longer and end the conversation, leaving everyone frustrated.

Assessing the quality of interaction correctly is therefore crucial for being able to respond appropriately and for contributing to communication being as productive as possible.

Do not Try to be Polite, Try to Support Transformation

Sometimes trying to be polite is an obstacle to conflict transformation. Sometimes the approach that brings transformation seems to be at odds with politeness. For example: I should not interfere in conversation or I should not interrupt the one that is speaking.

If, for example, a mediator is hesitant to intervene in the conversation (in a transformative way), he will not be able to do his job. And if we always wait for the others to stop speaking, we may wait for a long time while the other person starts repeating himself or lists less important details that support the initial position, which may in turn contribute to less constructive interaction.

Constructive interaction is not always polite and polite interaction is not always constructive, and it is important to be able to distinguish between the two.

Intrapersonal transformative communication skills
• Assessing One's Own Internal Strength
• Distancing Oneself from the Speaker's Statement
• Regaining Internal Stability
• Assessing the Internal State of Strength of the Other
• Assessing the Quality of Interaction
• Do not Try to be Polite, Try to Support Transformation

Table 3: Intrapersonal transformative communication skills

2. Conflict and Mediation

Mediation is a very useful tool for managing conflicts in relationships, organizations or communities. There are different types of mediation in relation to the model of mediation used and there are different types of mediation in relation to the stages of conflict. Namely mediation can be used at a very early stage of the conflict or it can be used late when the conflict has become more severe, even when there are already severe negative consequences of conflict.

It is very beneficial for the company or organization if it has implemented a system of in-house mediation because it can attend to and successfully deal with conflicts at early stages. However, in addition to mediation, there is a need for a more general system and commitment to effectively manage and prevent conflict, as well as to maintain a high quality of communication in an organization or community.

Transformative Mediation

In general, mediation is defined as a process where a neutral third party (mediator) assists parties in conflict to clarify misunderstanding and come to mutually agreeable solution. The goal of mediation from transformative perspective, however, is to change interaction from destructive to constructive. Ideally, parties in conflict would do that themselves, however, sometimes parties are not able to do that on their own, so a neutral third party can be very helpful in this respect.

Transformative mediation is therefore a process in which a third party works with parties in conflict to help them change the quality of their conflict interaction from negative and destructive to positive and constructive, as they discuss and explore issues and possibilities for resolution (Bush & Folger, 2005, pp.65-66).

The Role of the Transformative Mediator

A mediator with a "transformative" orientation starts from relational premises and believes that parties in conflict want most of all to change (transform) their interaction with each other from destructive to constructive, while they explore various topics and possibilities for resolution.

The mediator's job is therefore to help the parties achieve such a change, by supporting them in making empowerment and recognition shifts; helping the parties to transform their interaction. If mediators do this job, parties are likely to make positive changes in their interactions and, as a result, find acceptable terms of resolution for themselves when and where such terms genuinely exist (ISCT, 2012).

Mediator's Neutrality

The mediator should be neutral as to content and outcome of mediation. But it is not enough that the mediators do not share their opinion with the clients but they must be able to set their thoughts aside and focus on the process of communication, otherwise their position could impact their way of intervention and could, without realizing, impact the process and the contents of the conversation and potentially prevent the successful outcome of mediation. If not trained differently, people tend to adopt the attitude or position on contents they are perceiving (even if they are not aware). So how does a mediator manage not only not to give his or her opinions but also to set them aside? The answer is in focusing on the process of communication and supporting empowerment and recognition shifts which are changing the quality of interaction from negative and destructive to positive and constructive, which helps preserve neutrality.

Should Mediation be Voluntary?

One of the basic principles of mediation is voluntariness. If parties are free to choose and design their own solution, it is more likely that the solution will be honored than if it is somebody else who decides. However, that does not mean that parties should always be free to choose whether to go to mediation or not, especially if their conflict affects other people (coworkers, company, children, etc.), which is so often the case. If conflict affects other people, there should be a mechanism in place to require parties to sort out their disagreement, as well as support available for that process.

In terms of voluntariness we can observe at least three aspects, namely: 1. voluntary agreement, 2. voluntary cooperation and 3. voluntary arrival.

1. Voluntary agreement means that parties agree on a solution because they choose to and not because they are so ordered or forced, and that the content of the agreement is chosen by the parties.
2. Voluntary cooperation means that parties are free to decide what they will tell or not tell, how active or passive they will be and what, if any, proposals they will give.
3. And voluntary arrival means that parties come to mediation because they choose to and because they want to resolve a certain issue through constructive conversation to the satisfaction of both.

From the mediator's point of view all three aspects should be voluntary. However, that does not mean, for example, that parties are not sent to mediation and that a request is not made to sort some things out. And if parties did not decide to come to mediation on their own, that does not mean that the mediator will end mediation or refuse parties just because they did not come out of their free will. It means, however, that he/she will treat them as if they did but also acknowledge the fact that they did not choose to and help them decide what they want to do about it.

In terms of voluntary cooperation, parties are likely to start cooperating if the mediator knows what he or she is doing, since there probably is a conflict between them and conflict represents, in most cases, intense energy which 'forces' parties to respond (although destructively most of the time) to the other party as the mediator has the necessary skills to deal effectively with the situation. So, it is the very existence of a conflict that contributes to the parties cooperating when in mediation.

Even if they do not come because they chose to, certainly the agreement, if reached, should be voluntary. Namely parties have to want to agree and should be able to decide on the terms of their agreement. So even if they were required to do so, it is up to them how they do it. But if the mediator does his job well, he helps the parties change the quality of their interaction and consequently enables them to reach a solution that they agree with.

Models of Mediation Practice

There are obviously different models of mediation. In this book the transformative model of mediation is presupposed. That does not mean, however, that other models of mediation should not be used in general but it does mean that, in the context of communication wellness, the transformative model is most suited for the task since it focuses precisely on the quality of interaction that is the essence of communication wellness. A comparison of two main approaches is presented in the table below (Table 4), namely the transformative approach and the facilitative approach.

Model:	Transformative	Facilitative
Conflict is:	Crisis in human interaction	Problem in needs-satisfaction
Successful outcome of conflict intervention:	Shifts from destructive to constructive interaction between the parties; Increased capacity of the parties for future decision-making and communication	Settlement agreement that solves the problem on fair, realistic terms
Goal of third-party intervention:	Foster empowerment and recognition; Enhance party decision-making and communication; Help change interaction from destructive to constructive	Encourage interest-based bargaining; Generate an agreement that resolves tangible issues
Practice hallmarks:	Micro-focus on interaction; Identify opportunities for empowerment of the parties and inter-party recognition; Support deliberation & decision- making of the parties, and inter-party perspective-taking	Macro-focus: form global assessments of "problem"; Shape settlement terms; Drop "intangible" issues

Table 4: Comparison between transformative and facilitative model of mediation (ISCT, 2012)

The key difference lies in what is the primary goal of mediation and therefore the task of the mediator. Is it the settlement or practical resolution of the issue (facilitative model) or is it a change in quality of

43

interaction from destructive to constructive (transformative model)? In both cases, the other outcome is also appreciated but it is not the main goal. So, where is the problem?

Depending on the primary goal, the mediator also chooses his or her approach and the tools to do the task. And sometimes in pursuing the settlement, opportunities for transformation (which is not the primary goal) are overlooked or ignored. Consequently, the solution or settlement reached might be practical but the conflict between the parties remains. Other times, however, it is precisely due to the of lack of transformation that not even a solution or settlement can be reached.

On the other hand, if the primary goal is transformation, that is a change in the quality of interaction, the mediator consciously looks for and supports opportunities for empowerment and recognition when parties are discussing the issue at hand. It is this effort which gradually helps them change the quality of interaction for the better, which makes it easier for them to cooperate and search for a solution. So, if transformation occurs and a solution is possible, parties are most likely to be able to find or create a satisfactory solution for themselves without the mediator directly helping with it.

Obviously, there are other models of mediation practice, for example, evaluative, narrative, directive, therapeutic and others. And there are also mixed approaches which combine tools of different approaches. In any case, we can look at them in terms of what is the primary goal of the mediator: settlement or transformation.

Curative, Preventive and Proactive Conflict Mediation

Mediation as intervention can be used at any stage of conflict as presented below and indeed even if there is no conflict. The sooner the better is true in this context for at least two reasons:

1. If we use mediation in early stages of conflict, we can put in less time (and money) and energy for a successful outcome and we generally get more satisfying results.
2. The longer we wait in using mediation for dealing with conflicts, the longer we are paying the price of unresolved conflicts which are taking their toll on the quality of communication, relationships, efficiency, motivation, atmosphere, etc.

Curative mediation refers to use of mediation when a conflict has already taken a heavy toll, either in terms of health, broken relationships, formal proceedings, including lawsuits, etc. The function of mediation at this stage is elimination of conflict consequences, ending formal proceedings consensually or managing broken relationships. Court-annexed mediation, for example, is purely curative, meaning it deals with difficult consequences of conflict, since it is used very late in the process of conflict escalation.

Preventive mediation refers to the use of mediation one step earlier. The conflict has already taken a big toll but worse consequences can still be prevented. Lawsuits can be avoided, relationships can be saved, health preserved, etc. The function of mediation at this stage is managing unresolved issues and preventing further conflict escalation and/or relationship breakdown.

Proactive mediation, however, takes place before conflicts would take a big a toll. It is used as soon as indications of conflict are present or even when the less optimal functioning of a team is observed. The function of mediation, if used at this stage, is improvement of the relationship and better cooperation in relationships or groups which are already good.

Proactive mediation	Preventive mediation	Curative mediation
Good relationships with some unresolved issues	Relationships with **some difficult conflicts**, possibly on the verge of break-up	Relationships where **heavy consequences of conflict** are already showing or broken-up relationships
Purpose Improvement of relationships and better cooperation in personal or work-place relationships which are already good	**Purpose** Managing unresolved issues and preventing conflict escalation and/or relationship breakdown	**Purpose** Elimination of conflict consequences or managing broken relationships

Table 5: Proactive, preventive and curative mediation (Iršič, 2010)

After a speech at an international conference of mediators where I also presented this model, a colleague mediator came to me and said: 'You know what? I realized that I am only doing curative mediation!'

In-house Mediation

In-house mediation is a service organized by the company or organization which offers mediation to its employees in case of disputes. Chosen employees or members of the staff are trained as mediators and available to offer support in case of conflicts. Most of the time they are not only mediators but mediation is part of their job description.

There are a variety of designs in terms of in-house mediation services. 1. There can be one trained mediator in the company. 2. There can be a list of trained mediators available to choose from. 3. There can be a team of mediators with a mediation coordinator responsible for organizing mediation 4. In addition to the existence of the team and the coordinator all employees are informed about the existence and benefits of using mediation services.

Obviously the fourth design is the most efficient in terms of contributing to the quality of communication but nevertheless mediation, even if internal, is perceived as a service for difficult issues (e.g. relationship breakdown, harassment, discrimination, bullying, etc.) or a service for settling legal disputes. To be fair, most of the time it is also branded that way, especially by lawyer mediators. Consequently, many companies do not even use mediation because they believe they do not have any problems that are suitable for mediation.

Obviously, if their perception of mediation is a help for settling legal disputes or a service for handling difficult issues and they do not see mediation as transformative support for constructive communication, the fact that it is seldom used is not surprising.

Why Mediation is not Enough

Although mediation (especially the transformative model) is a magnificent tool for the quality of communication, many people do not decide to use it. And there are multiple reasons for that.

In my opinion, there are four main reasons for not using (transformative) mediation as a support or help with resolving conflicts more frequently.

One is a **lack of awareness and understanding of how transformative mediation works** and a lack of information about transformative mediation as such. Additionally, there is the lack of experience with such intervention in general. It is not commonly used and third parties that witness conflict usually do not know how to help effectively.

The second reason is that people **when in conflict usually perceive that the conflict is the other party's fault**, that the other party is responsible for the fact that conflict occurred. When in conflict, they perceive the other party as causing problems or difficulties and therefore talking to the other party does not seem so appealing even with the help of a mediator. Using the words of someone to explain why he would never consider mediation: »If the other party is so difficult that we cannot resolve our difference ourselves, no mediator is going to be able to help! «

Participation in mediation, or trying to solve interpersonal conflicts **using mediation, means a great personal investment**. It means that a great personal involvement is required in order to be able to resolve the conflict. Among others, it means that parties must be willing to discuss their situation, to try to perceive the situation from a different perspective, to try to express what they need or consider valuable and to be open to discover something new in terms of understanding and the possibilities which were not seen before. Furthermore, being vulnerable to a certain extent and a risk of being hurt (again) is common when conflict issues are discussed.

A lack of good examples or practice of conflict being successfully resolved, either using mediation or by parties themselves, is the fourth reason. It is not everyday experience that conflicts lead to improvement. It is oftentimes the opposite. When conflict occurs, it normally means that the relationship became worse and represents the first step towards deterioration or even ending the relationship rather than an opportunity for growth, which conflict is supposed to be.

But it is the lack of common experience with conflicts actually bringing improvement of either relationship or personal growth that also makes mediation less appealing. It would be different if it were common experience that when conflict occurs, either the parties themselves or by using mediation they transform the situation and actually gain a lot of benefits from the conflict. In such a case, the use of mediation would also sooner rather than later become more appealing. But for the time being this is not the case and consequently parties in conflict are not so motivated or attracted to using mediation.

Furthermore, conflicts are often suppressed or ignored (often due to the lack of awareness of their presence, impact and dynamics and the lack of appropriate skills). On the other hand, there is concern *What if it gets worse?*, so people postpone dealing with them. Consequently, they are dealt with when they already escalate and are so much harder to transform or resolve. People also often feel, that they "do not need help" with communication and that they "do not have conflicts".

Many times people do not even think about using mediation because:

- It does not occur to them that they could use mediation
- They do not recognize situations where mediation could be useful
- They do not have good communication with the person they could propose mediation to
- They feel that issues are not big enough to require mediation ("It is not a big deal!")
- They feel that conflict is too severe to be able to resolve with mediation
- There is physical or geographical distance and/or lack of technological tools
- There are financial issues ("Who is going to pay for it?")
- There is subconscious fear to confront oneself and realize that they are contributing to the problem
- They are afraid it could get worse
- They do not like the other party
- etc.

Even if they consider mediation, people often do not propose it to the other party (personally or through a mediation center) because:

- They assume that the other party will refuse a proposal for mediation
- They assume that mediation will not be successful
- They do not see how the situation could be resolved ('What can we possibly solve?')
- They do not trust that other party would be willing to cooperate in searching for the solution or even listen
- They are worried that the other party may misunderstand a proposal for mediation (e.g. as a sign of severe conflict or a sign of weakness etc.)
- etc.

Mediation is in general perceived as a tool for dealing with conflicts and conflicts are still widely perceived as failure. 'Successful people do not have conflicts' is a myth which prevents less successful people from getting help in the early stages for fear of being perceived as unsuccessful. Successful people, however, are better at dealing with conflicts, either by themselves or by professional support. They in general also have a higher conflict tolerance and are therefore able to prosper in spite of conflicts they are facing or even due to conflicts they manage to transform.

In general, conflicts are not recognized as an opportunity for growth nor as a fact of life, therefore they are often avoided and not dealt with appropriately. Consequently, besides the fact that it represents additional costs, mediation is generally postponed to later stages of conflict, many times to the curative phase (e.g. when the dispute is taken to the court) and often it is not used even then if not ordered or demanded.

3. Stages of Conflict

There are different stages of conflict escalation. Below Glasl's nine-stage model is presented and thereafter a six-stage model of conflict transformation is proposed. Additionally, three levels of conflict management in relation to the consequences of conflict are discussed.

Glasl's Nine-Stage Model of Conflict Escalation

Friedrich Glasl (Glasl, 1999; Jordan, 2000) describes the escalation of destructive conflict through nine stages which lead one to another if not reversed. The stages which are briefly described below are: 1. Hardening, 2. Debates and polemics, 3. Actions not words, 4. Images and coalitions; 5. Loss of face, 6. Strategies of threats, 7. Limited destructive blows, 8. Fragmentation of the enemy and 9. Together into the abyss.

Stage 1: Hardening

The first stage occurs when there is a difference over some issue or frustration in a relationship which is resistant to resolution efforts. Attempts at dealing with the difficulties repeatedly fail. The parties are not able to sort out the issues by themselves. Each party progressively adopts fixed positions regarding the issue. The positions are perceived mutually incompatible by the parties.

If other people are present groups start to form around positions. Members of each party are strongly susceptible to negative information about the other party. Negative information is given great significance and positive information is not integrated.

Interactions with the other side bring no progress and are perceived as a waste of time and energy and the other party is perceived as stubborn and unreasonable. Despite that, parties are still trying to come to terms with the other side and be fair.

Stage 2: Debates and Polemics

The second stage begins when one or both parties lose faith that rational discussion would bring results. Since the rational argumentation does not seem to bring results, discussions change into confrontations. Parties adopt increasingly rigid positions. The goal is to push through one's own standpoint. Interactions change from rational arguments towards emotions and relative power issues. The discussions are about who is right rather than what is right.

When rational and relevant arguments are not successful, parties resort to "quasi-rational" argumentation, such as: bickering about the underlying causes, strong exaggeration of the implications and consequences of the counterpart's position, linking the issue to larger value considerations, reference to recognized authorities, stating the alternatives as extremes, etc.

The parties expect each other to try to gain advantages at the other's expense. The growing mistrust creates a sense of insecurity and loss of control. The tension builds up and occasional outbursts let out the pressure but do not contribute towards solving the problem.

Stage 3: Actions, not Words

When one party feels that further talking is useless and starts acting without consulting the other side, the conflict slips into stage three. The parties feel blocked by the other side and perceive each other as competitors rather than working for common goals. They try to gain the upper hand and make the other side dependent on them. They try to prevent the other side from reaching their goal since that could prevent them from reaching their own.

Action and non-verbal communication, rather than discussion, are employed and consequently the escalation process is enhanced. Parties perceive themselves as being restricted by the situation over which they have no control and consequently reject responsibility for their own actions. Their actions are perceived merely as only possible response to the actions of the other side.

There is increased pressure within each side to be unified and to perceive things the same way at the expense of internal diversity and accurate assessment of reality.

Stage 4: Images and Coalitions

At stage four the conflict is no longer about concrete issues but about victory or defeat. Defending one's reputation is a major concern. General and stereotypical negative images of the counterpart are formed. They are very resistant to change and impact the perception of the other. They prevent the parties from seeing each other's complexity and individuality. Each side tries to impose their perception of the other but at the same time refuses the image the other side holds of them. It becomes increasingly difficult for the parties to mention positive qualities of the counterpart even if asked.

A typical form of interaction at this stage is "deniable punishment behavior." The counterpart is subtly provoked, insulted and criticized. Insinuations, ambiguous comments, irony and body language are used but the perpetrator can deny that any harm was intended, if challenged. Since the other party cannot openly discuss the incidents, they are very likely to respond in kind. The goal of each side is to defeat the other and not to resolve the dispute. Attacks are made on the identity, attitude, behavior, position and relationships of the counterpart. The source of conflict is considered to be the other side and not the differences or incompatibilities.

The parties are actively seeking support from others and are consciously bringing out their differences in public in order to gain support for their position.

Stage 5: Loss of Face

At stage five the parties in conflict feel that they have suddenly seen through the mask of the other party and discovered an immoral, insane or criminal inside. It appears as a sudden insight into the true and very different nature of the other: „Finally they show their true face. "

The whole conflict history is seen from a different perspective: possible constructive actions are understood as deceptions and destructive actions are considered as true representations of other's intentions and the true nature of the other. The distinction between parties is no longer in terms better and worse but in terms good and evil. Each side considers themselves as good and the other as evil that has to be defeated.

Stage 6: Strategies of Threats

In this phase, parties start to use threats against the other side in order to prevail. There are three increasing phases of issuing threats: 1. Parties issue mutual threats in order to show that they will not retreat. 2. Threats are made more concrete, unequivocal and firm. 3. Threats are formulated as an ultimatum.

In this phase, the conflict becomes increasingly complex, difficult to grasp and impossible to control. Threats increase pressure on each side that diminishes the possibility of conscious deliberation and consideration of alternative possibilities. The situation is perceived as dangerous and chaotic. The behavior becomes impulsive and aiming for strong effect. At this stage, taking the story to the media is common.

Public declarations or smaller aggressive acts that are intended to show credibility of threats are perceived by the other party as proof of aggressive intentions and the capabilities of the opponent. Consequently, they 'fight back', which is in turn perceived as proof of their aggressive intentions. By resorting to threats, parties restrict themselves from choosing a more productive approach. The very internal dynamics of stage six drive the parties to translate the threats into action.

Stage 7: Limited Destructive Blows

The threats of stage six undermine the basic sense of security of the parties. Each side perceives the other as hostile and capable of destructive acts. Preserving their own safety and survival becomes the key focus. Parties do not see the possibility of solution that would include the other but seek to eliminate the enemy which, in their eyes, no longer has human characteristics.

The attacks lead to retaliations, often even more destructive. Even though losses of the enemy do not bring any benefits, they are perceived as gains or successful action. Even at the expense of one's own losses, the parties are striving to damage the enemy as long as the enemy's losses are greater. Parties do not strive for victory any longer but aim for survival and suffering less damage than the enemy.

Stage 8: Fragmentation of the Enemy

At this stage the attacks intensify and aim at destroying the vital systems and the basis of power of the enemy. Strong efforts at suppressing internal conflicts are employed. This increases stress and internal pressure within the parties, which channels into more intense actions aimed against the other side. On the other hand, conflicts within each side intensify as well, which only adds to the chaos. The attacks are aimed at vital parts of the other side with the aim of destroying the enemy. The only limitation is preserving one's own survival.

Stage 9: Together into the Abyss

At the last stage of conflict escalation, the drive to destroy the enemy is so intense that even their own survival is not an obstacle any more. The enemy must be destroyed even at the expense of one's own destruction.

Stages of Productive Conflict Interaction

Each conflict presents a challenge to the quality of communication and satisfaction with the relationship. If the interaction spirals down, there is danger of damage as described above. However, if, when faced with conflict, interaction is constructive, conflict can bring improvement and growth. As opposed to the nine-stage model of destructive conflict escalation described above, we propose below a model of stages of productive conflict interaction based on observation of many successfully resolved conflict situations and many transformative conversations. The model proposed and described here does not in any way contradict Glasl's observations or model. It differs strongly merely because it models a different kind of interaction.

Stage 1: Disruption in Communication

In order to be able to speak about conflict, there has to be at least some sort of disruption in interaction, cooperation or communication. If everything is harmonious, we cannot speak about conflict. Stage one therefore starts with the existence of any disruption in communication, cooperation or interaction. The difficulty persists since strategies and behaviors which are functional in harmony tend to be dysfunctional in conflict (e.g. explaining and clarifying one's own position or proposal) and the conflict impacts our perceptions, thoughts and feelings. Due to this change, we tend to subconsciously ascribe the reason for disruption to the other, which only contributes to conflict escalation. Frustration is a common feeling at this stage.

Stage 2: Acceptance of Conflict

Stage two starts when at least one party (it can also be the mediator) flips their perception and becomes aware of interactional difficulty. Nothing changes yet but the situation is perceived at least by one party as conflict that should be dealt with constructively or in a different way than it is being dealt with. It can also be accompanied with a declaration or labeling of the situation (e.g. *It seems we disagree. We have a conflict. Let us try to work it out.*, etc.) The awareness of conflict can spread to other(s) or not but for those who accept the fact that there is conflict, perception of the situation and their inner state changes. At least a slight increase of the sense of clarity and an increase of the inner feeling of stability are characteristic of this stage for those who become aware of the conflict.

Stage 3: Conscious Efforts

Stage three begins when conscious efforts to transform conflict start at least by one participant (again it can also be the mediator or a non-formal mediator). Obviously, it works better if more or all of the people involved do so but it suffices also if at least one starts. Conscious effort can include using skills described in chapter one (reflection, summary and checking in) and consequently all involved gradually become more empowered. It is a feeling of strong engagement and focus, as in solving a difficult task, that is characteristic of this stage.

Stage 4: Clarification and Understanding

If conscious efforts are successful, they lead to gradual clarification and changes in understanding of the situation, oneself and also the other. Tension which is characteristic of escalation decreases.

Interaction becomes lighter and more conscious. There is gradually more space and time and understanding for each participant and each participant's views are better understood. There is an improved sense of clarity and understanding and some sense of relief since the conflict has become more manageable.

Stage 5: Agreement and Appreciation of Differences

In stage five parties come to realize that there is a lot they agree on and at the same time they appreciate and allow the differences between them. They find or create options which would be acceptable to all, based on the new understanding of the situation, themselves and each other and work out possibilities for allowing differences to remain and be accepted. A feeling of being on the same side and working together is present.

Stage 6: Excitement and Affection

Stage six begins when issues have been sorted out successfully at least for the most part and both/all parties feel they were understood and taken into account. Life is back to normal but with added quality. Parties feel they are treated with kindness or generosity and they reciprocate that attitude. Their affection for the other party changes for the better and they feel some excitement about transcending the conflict.

Spontaneous Conflict Transformation and Transfor-mative Communication

Obviously, a similar process can also happen without conscious effort and acceptance of conflict but it would be guided more intuitively rather than consciously. Nevertheless, it still corresponds to the same stages of productive conflict interaction and has value in itself even if it is not noticed. This happens many times spontaneously without knowing it and we do not notice it precisely because it ends well. The more so if the general level of communication between parties is good and the difficulty of the issue or disruption is low.

It can also happen that interaction corresponds only to the last three levels, that is: 4. clarification and understanding, 5.agreement and appreciation of differences and 6. excitement and affection. In such cases, we would not consider it as conflict transformation but rather as (spontaneous) transformative communication. It cannot be considered as conflict if there is no disruption of any sort but benefits of the transformative process can occur nevertheless.

Incomplete Set of Stages

It is important to note that the stages described above are far from being linear or discrete. There can be much overlapping and also falling back when a new issue is discovered and it can be multilayered, that is at different stages with respect to different issues or layers of communication. At the same time, there is a positive overall trend in terms of changing interaction for the better and each new issue is more likely to be sorted out more easily.

In addition, the stages described represent an ideal pattern which does not always occur in its entirety for different reasons. Either the process is interrupted or there is not enough time or the support available is not sufficient or the conflict is too difficult and too complex, etc., so it may well be that in spite of all efforts we will not always reach stage six (excitement and affection), which does not mean, however, that the efforts were fruitless since the effects of a constructive interaction (as well as those of destructive) accumulate in the long run.

For example, at one point in the conflict situation we become aware of the conflict (stage two). Even if the situation plays out as usual, there is the added quality in that situation, namely we gained insight about it. And we can think about how to respond next time rather than feeling frustrated. Also, we can deliberate if it is appropriate to propose some kind of transformative support or to talk about it later. All those choices and conscious deliberation can already have empowering effect on us, even if nothing else changes. The same goes if we manage to put in some conscious effort to transform conflict but it fails. In addition to being aware we also did something differently. Again, we can think about the situation and analyze it rather than feeling helpless and we can learn from that and devise a better plan for next time. Furthermore, by consciously trying to do things differently, we gain experience and practice skills (even if we fail) required for successful conflict transformation.

Curative, Preventive and Proactive Conflict Management

As described in the previous chapter there are different types of mediation with respect to conflict escalation: curative, preventive and proactive. This refers to how soon in the process of conflict escalation we use mediation. Similarly, we can observe the starting points for trying to manage the conflict constructively regardless of the way we do it in relation to severity of the consequences of conflict.

Regardless of whether parties do it themselves, there is non-formal support or a formal process of managing conflict, it plays a major role when people start handling conflict as such. The earlier the better is a general rule. However, the reality is oftentimes opposite, since people tend to avoid, ignore or endure conflict too long and often until they can no longer bear it. Especially, the formal processes of managing conflicts are postponed to the stage when it really is high time to deal with them.

Curative Conflict Management

Curative conflict management refers to dealing with conflict late in the process when there are already severe consequences present (ending cooperation, lawsuit, harassment complaint, health issues, loss of income, loss of good reputation, etc.). Most of the time it involves also some sort of formal procedures (e.g. mediation, formal complaint, court proceedings, etc.). By the time steps towards managing the conflict are taken, the price (financial and nonfinancial) is very high.

Preventive Conflict Management

One stage earlier, when the worst consequences of conflict can still be avoided, we can talk about preventive conflict management aimed at managing the situation and preventing further deterioration of the situation. Even if not so severe, consequences of conflict are still very serious. Preventive conflict management can involve formal processes (e.g. mediation, counseling, training, etc.), as well as less formal processes (e.g. coaching, dialogue, etc.) or non-formal processes (e.g. transformative communication, non-formal mediation, etc.)

Proactive Conflict Management

Proactive conflict management on the other hand refers to dealing with conflicts when some might not even perceive the situation as conflict and, indeed, there need not be a conflict at all. It suffices that there is disruption of interaction of any sort. There is however still plenty of reserve, so most of the time it is even not necessary to deal with the situation on the spot. At the proactive stage less formal processes of managing conflicts are predominant. In addition to using transformative communication skills, 'on the spot mediation', communication first aid, non-formal mediation, transformative conversation, transformative coaching and others can be employed.

Detecting and Dealing with Conflict at Early Stages

The key to proactive conflict management is to detect disruption early enough and to deal with it appropriately. By that, however, I do not mean to make a drama out of every little thing but to attend to it and sort it out to the satisfaction of all.

Like a person who has a very tidy place. They detect every little 'disruption in the order and cleanliness'. They do not make a drama but they notice it and sort it out (either themselves or by hired help). Or a good mechanic who can tell you what is wrong with the car already by the sound of the engine, long before anything breaks down.

He can predict and prevent difficulties long before they become detrimental.

It is important therefore to be able to detect, while still being perfectly fine, the disruption in communication and to sort it out before it hurts the relationship or organization.

It helps to have a tool or a method for assessing the quality of interaction among parties and a way of detecting 'disruptions'. One such tool is presented in chapter six where three sets of questions which can be used as questionnaires are presented.

Many times people notice disruption but since they do not know what to do about it they just accept it (in terms of: we are different or not everyone can get along well, etc.) or do not want to get involved in it in order not to make things worse or not to get caught in the middle. Such approach, however, hurts the relationship in the long run, as well as the organization as a whole.

4. Conflict Resiliency

There is no such thing as a conflict free relationship or organization. But there are differences in how individuals and organizations deal with conflicts. One aspect relevant to a successful relationship or organization is conflict resiliency. Conflict resiliency can be considered as the capacity of individuals (we will also present the concept of conflict competence in this respect) but also as a trait of a group or organization in terms of how does a whole respond to conflict that appears between its members.

In this chapter, we will briefly discuss the characteristics of a conflict resilient workplace, present conflict competence that is characteristic of individuals who are better able to deal with conflicts and present the 'mapping approach' to communication which makes it easier to understand what is happening in terms of conflict and communication in order to be more clear on what is going on, what needs to change and how to do it.

All three aspects (organizational, individual and conceptual) have to be developed in order to achieve optimal results.

To illustrate, even if an individual has a very high conflict competence but the organization does not encourage nor allow or provide opportunities to deal with conflicts constructively, this fact has an undermining effect on the success of dealing with conflicts.

Similarly, if conflicts are not perceived as situations that have to and can be dealt with in terms of changing interaction, but are perceived as a general incompatibility of individuals or even caused by one side which is more inclined to conflict, the outcome will be very different, even if the organization supports conflict resolution processes.

Furthermore, if conflicts are perceived as crises in interaction and there exist opportunities and support for managing conflicts but if individuals have very low conflict competence, the benefits of the before mentioned factors will not be as strong as if individuals possessed a high level of conflict competence.

A Conflict Resilient Workplace

A Conflict resilient workplace does not mean a workplace without conflicts but a workplace **where conflicts are dealt with appropriately and early on.** It means that there exist opportunities and options for dealing with conflicts constructively at the workplace, known to all, and that using them is also encouraged. There are several characteristics of a conflict resilient workplaces:

1. Owners and leadership consider good communication and relationships, as well as dealing constructively with conflicts, important.
2. Organization and work procedures are set so that they do not produce confusion or conflict themselves and mechanisms are in place for optimizing the system if sources of disruption are discovered within.
3. Employees are encouraged and trained on how to deal constructively with conflicts by themselves in the first place and

are also informed and trained on how to search for support when they fail to sort out the conflict by themselves.

4. Several options for support in dealing with conflicts are available for workers (including informal, semiformal, as well as formal processes) and workers are informed and trained on how and when to use them.

5. There are procedures and criteria on how to detect possible conflict early on by third parties and all are also aware of how to act when they notice indications of conflict.

6. Quality communication and good relationships are valued, fostered and promoted and training courses are provided in order to develop skills that contribute to building high-quality relationships and good communication.

7. Early response to dealing with conflicts is encouraged and valued and employees are aware of dangers and damaging consequences of conflict escalation and motivated to contribute to early conflict management.

8. Some support for personal problems or situations of employees is available in order for the employees to be able to work out their personal situations and prevent negative impact of personal situation to work context.

Conflict Competence

Conflict competence is an acquired capacity of the individual to sense and recognize conflicts and to be able to deal with them constructively. It comprises two elements, namely conflict sensitivity and conflict tolerance, which are presented below. A study conducted by Rakmo Institute in 2016 revealed a correlation between conflict competence and physical health, psychological health and satisfaction at the workplace. The following pages briefly present the key aspects of conflict competence, namely conflict tolerance and conflict sensitivity. A more detailed elaboration is presented in the book Conflict Competence: Understanding, Assessing and Improving the Ability to Deal with Conflicts (Iršič, 2017).

Conflict Tolerance

Conflict tolerance is the ability to function constructively even if there is conflict. The higher conflict tolerance the more conflict one is able to endure and preserve constructive behavior. The threshold is reached when responses of an individual stop being constructive (e.g. stops listening, starts attacking the other, behaves defensively, bursts out, etc.).

Conflict tolerance includes the ability to: function in spite of conflict; drop less important issues; disregard smaller conflicts; understand smaller conflicts as information or means of communication; postpone dealing with particular issue; 'switch' to another activity without negative impact of conflict; 'switch' to meta level of communication and the ability to ignore negative aspects of interaction and respond to positive ones when communication includes both.

Conflict tolerance can be regarded as one's general capacity, that is how well he or she handles the 'heat of the conflict' in general but also as a current level of tolerance which varies in relation to different people, contexts, situations and one's own state.

Current level of conflict tolerance is influenced by several factors including:

- Context (people or environment)
- Situation
- Previously (un)resolved conflicts in a particular relationship and in general
- Mood and emotional state (happy, optimistic, sad, angry, afraid, worried, etc.)
- Physiological state (tired, ill, hungry, sleepy, etc.)
- Transitions and change (coming home, arriving to work, etc.)

It is important to be aware of the changing nature of conflict tolerance and one's own current state since when our tolerance is decreased, it is possible and wise to postpone dealing with a particular issue, which increases the chances that it will be resolved successfully.

We can improve our conflict tolerance by getting used to (smaller) conflicts (in terms not being afraid of them) and acquiring and practicing skills for dealing with conflicts (at training courses, workshops, with colleagues, on our own by mental practice or in real situations where we apply appropriate skills). Furthermore, individual or joint analysis of the interaction and outcome of both successfully resolved and unresolved conflicts is very functional in this respect.

In addition to acquiring and practicing skills, each successfully resolved conflict (even if small) contributes to increased conflict tolerance especially in the same relationship or context. Additional means to improve conflict tolerance are changing the perspective (e.g. looking at the same situation from the future) or a broader context (seeing the conflict situation together with other aspects and situations, in particular the relationship or the environment).

Conflict sensitivity

Conflict sensitivity refers to the ability of individuals to sense and recognize a conflict in interactions or relationships. Conflict sensitivity includes awareness about the existence of conflicts, the ability (and willingness) to sense and recognize conflicts when interaction is hindered, the ability to foresee conflicts which may occur, the ability to analyze development and elements of conflict, the ability to consider different meanings, points of view, convictions, positions and value systems, and the ability to notice different understanding or interpretations.

Conflict sensitivity can be systematically improved by (self)observation and analysis of our own conflicts (successfully resolved and also unresolved) or those we witness either in our surroundings or in movies, literature, talk shows, news etc., learning (through books, articles, videos, seminars, workshops and training courses), practical, written (e.g. transcribing conflict interaction) or mental exercises.

All the above expand and differentiate our understanding and awareness of conflicts and related concepts and phenomena, and consequently improve our conflict sensitivity.

Assessing Conflict Competence

Conflict competence of individuals, as well as that of organizations can be assessed in various ways. One of them is using the questionnaire that I developed comprising 48 questions which measure conflict sensitivity and conflict tolerance, out of which the score result for conflict competence is calculated. If administered to a group, conflict competence of a group can be calculated and analyzed as well.

It is presented and its use described in more detail in the book entitled Conflict Competence: Understanding, Assessing and Improving the Ability to Deal with Conflicts (Iršič, 2017) and it measures separately conflict tolerance and conflict sensitivity, as well as combined conflict competence.

If conflict competence is less than optimal, either one or both of the factors can be responsible. On the other hand, even if conflict competence is relatively high, one of the factors can still be suboptimal and consequently assessing that and working on improving it can have a huge impact on improving conflict competence in general.

Relation between Conflict Competence and Quality of Communication

Since unresolved conflicts are the main reason for the decrease in the quality of communication, higher conflict competence indicates a better quality of communication in general. Obviously, one has to take into account the variability of conflict tolerance from situation to situation, from relationship to relationship, and all factors that influence conflict tolerance, but nevertheless in general there is a correlation between a higher conflict competence and a higher quality of communication.

As already mentioned, research showed that people with higher conflict competence (measured with the questionnaire mentioned above) enjoy a higher level of both mental and physical health and also enjoy a higher level of job satisfaction than those with a lower level of conflict competence. More research needs to be done to clearly prove the relation between the level of conflict competence and the general quality of communication. It is safe to assume, however, that the higher the conflict competence, the higher the quality of communication in general.

Revisiting the Conflict/Communication Spiral

In chapter one we described a conflict spiral in the context of the transformative model of conflict and communication. The description in chapter one refers to a single situation which can be perceived in terms of constructive or destructive communication, which is particularly useful for observing a mediation or particular communication situation. In general, however, things are more complex and there are many contexts and situations, as well as issues, that have an impact on the quality of interaction.

A topic that parties strongly disagree about, for example, can quickly contribute to deterioration of communication. On the other hand, the same people can communicate or cooperate perfectly well in another area or on another topic. Sometimes certain topics (e.g. politics) are consciously avoided in order to preserve the quality of interaction and avoid destructive conflict. Other times, however, despite such an attempt or suggestion this does not succeed.

Normally we can relatively quickly restore the quality of interaction, either by changing topics, apologizing, calming down, adopting a more constructive attitude, changing interaction or by temporarily withdrawing from interaction with the same person and either talk to somebody else or start doing something else and then continue communication later, often as if nothing has happened.

The quality of interaction or relationship with a person whom we had a conflict with is normally not damaged by any particular incident. In the long run, however, the frequency and severity of 'disagreements' take their toll on the relationship, and overall quality and constructiveness of interaction with that person deteriorates. In more benign cases this shows merely in the avoidance of certain topics, and in less benign cases it represents a general negative precondition for interaction with that person in terms of starting future interactions on a lower level of quality to begin with.

Each interaction within a certain context (situation, person, topic) can be observed in terms of constructiveness or quality of communication, and we can 'map dangerous zones' of communication (particular topics with particular persons, particular situations, etc.) and then consciously decide how to deal with them.

Avoiding the engagement in communication on certain topics is sometimes very appropriate, especially if those topics do not directly affect our relationship or cooperation (e.g. politics). Avoiding communication about certain sensitive issues in a particular situation (e.g. if we are tired or if the other person is doing something else or is under pressure) is also very productive. It is also very wise to postpone certain discussions to a more appropriate time.

However, this strategy of avoiding or postponing is too often overused and consequently issues do not get resolved and we tend to become progressively anxious about communication on certain issues with a certain person, and in the long run, about communication with that person about anything meaningful to us. Consequently, failing to see our own contribution, as well as the interactional characteristics of that situation, we tend to ascribe the responsibility for that to the other person (e.g., *It is not possible to talk to her!* or *He is not capable of listening!*). The irony of that is of course that similar conclusions about the other come from both sides of the conflict.

Observing Our Communication and its Quality

To avoid outcomes as described above, it is wise to observe our communication more consciously also taking into account the topics or issues, the context or situation and the person we are talking to, on the one hand, and our inner sense of strength and wellbeing on the other. It is also beneficial to observe communication as such (e.g. constructive or destructive) and its impact on our own wellbeing and behavior, rather than focusing only on the other person's behavior and perceiving oneself (if communication is not constructive) as the other person's victim and them as aggressor.

Figure 2: Stages of the quality of communication in relation to constructiveness or destructiveness of interaction

The quality of communication regarding the same issue in the same situation with the same participants can change relatively quickly between high-quality communication, constructive conflict interaction, destructive conflict interaction and passive and active violence as illustrated above. Normally, people tend to interrupt interaction in the phase of destructive conflict or even violence and therefore prevent it from becoming even worse, which would most likely happen if they did not have appropriate skills or support. The unfortunate thing is, however, that they most of the time do not return to it in order to fix it (again due to the lack of skill or support) and consequently the general quality of their interaction gradually deteriorates.

The Field of Spirals

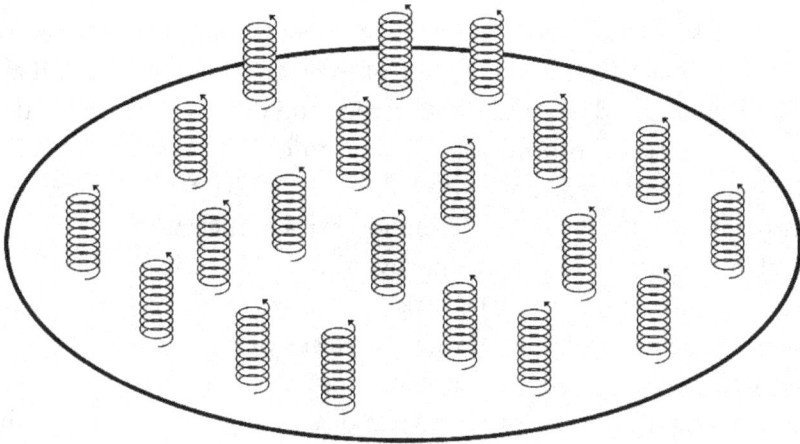

Figure 3: The field of spirals

We can imagine specific situations as spirals which have potential to be constructive or destructive. There are many such spirals in each relationship. Every time we engage in interaction about a certain issue, there is potential to make it better or worse. If we tend to leave the interaction at least the same or even better than it started, e.g., if we have a tendency to end conversations in a positive atmosphere, we will strengthen our capacity to talk constructively to the person concerned.

On the other hand, each communication that ends in a negative atmosphere contributes to the communication about that issue or even with that person being more challenging in the future and, using a metaphor, will present a hole in the communication field, which means that the spiral will begin on a slightly lower level of quality the next time.

Deciding on Priority to Keep Spirals Constructive

It is therefore well advised to decide to keep interaction constructive, or when we notice that it is not, to do something about it. There are at least three challenges related to that, namely, lack of awareness, lack of skill and lack of time.

Lack of awareness relates to not being consciously or semiconsciously alert to the quality of interaction all the time and also lack of understanding of the importance and dynamics of interaction, as well as lack of information on how to deal with situations when disruption is noticed. Lack of skill refers to the fact that generally people do not have conflict resolution skills sufficiently developed to be able to quickly restore or improve the quality of interaction when the disruption is noticed. And lack of time refers to the fact that with the overwhelming amount of work and tasks we have to attend to each day, combined with the desire that things would go smoothly, many times we have no time (or energy) to deal with another problem that pops up.

Even if we do not manage to end interaction constructively each time, we can still keep things in check and deal with them another time. A good tool to keep things in check is to map situations where things did not end well or they spiraled down in line with the guidelines below.

Mapping 'Communication Territory'

It is useful if we build a mental map of 'communication territory' together with its pitfalls (situations that are more likely to lead to destructive interaction), taking into account a combination of issues, situations, the other person and our inner state. People tend to do it intuitively and semiconsciously anyway but at that they tend to overgeneralize (e.g. *Communication with Tom is difficult. It is impossible to talk with him.*) rather than make it specific (e.g. *When talking to Tom* (person) *about reorganizing our responsibility* (issue) *which I was unhappy about* (inner state), *when he came to me to talk about the last month's project* (situation) *and seemed upset* (inner state of the other), *things got out of hand* (interaction) *and he walked away even more upset* (impact on the other) *and I was furious* (impact on self)).

The latter description is far more complex, analytical and objective than the first one and consequently much harder to do, especially if we are not used or trained to think that way, but on the other hand far more useful in helping us orient ourselves in 'communication territory' with that person or within a certain context or in general.

On the basis of our mental map (which we can also draw or write down to make it more conscious, explicit and useful) we can start adopting a conscious attitude towards certain topics within certain contexts – deciding whether to discuss or avoid or postpone them or (especially if they occur frequently an oftentimes contribute to decreasing communication quality) deciding on how to deal with them (e.g. going to mediation, point them out and ask for agreement on the time when it would be suitable to talk them through, etc.) .

Impact of Conflict on Others and Their Role

It is also well observed and documented that conflict has an impact on others (children, coworkers, customers, partners, etc.), that is to say, not only on those directly involved but also on those indirectly involved. The decrease of quality of interaction within one relationship can induce other conflict situations with others or at least make them feel less safe and less motivated than they would otherwise be.

It is therefore ill advised when noticing a conflict to just shrug one's shoulders saying: *They are not getting along well.* Or distancing oneself from the conflict (e.g. it is none of my concern) since it has a potential of damaging us or others eventually as well. However, it is also dangerous to get involved, especially if we are not trained to do so competently.

So, the question remains: what can we as observers do about it to help and not make it worse. We will discuss the options for intervention (e.g. referring to mediation) in more detail in chapter seven but for the time being let us at least establish that we do have a responsibility and a right to do something about it if not for another reason then because of its potential negative effect on us.

If we are not sure what to do about it, we can always turn to an in-house mediator or mediation coordinator (provided, of course, that the company has an in-house mediation service) in order to get support on that issue.

Should Dealing with Conflict be Voluntary?

Conflicts are seldom pleasant and due to various reasons people are neglecting, postponing or avoiding dealing with them, especially because of lack of skills, common practice, systemic encouragement and support for dealing with them.

On the other hand, there are various negative consequences of conflicts that are not dealt with as briefly described also in chapter five. Conflict, if not dealt with, gradually spreads and pollutes or even poisons (not unlike a contagious disease) the surroundings. Even in the most benign cases it still makes people uneasy and confused.

So, if conflict manifests itself in a certain context, there should be common practice that others are entitled to request from parties in conflict to deal with it appropriately. After all, even if it is a conflict that does not concern them directly, why would they have to be exposed to the presence of conflict between others and suffer a decrease of quality of atmosphere?

On the other hand, even if requested to do so, the way the parties sort out the conflict is still voluntary as discussed in chapter two. When given the opportunity to confront conflict, people respond or react to the actions of the other party whom they are in conflict with, and if there is transformative support offered, the transformation is likely to occur, and parties will be able to sort out the conflict in which they were trapped and were avoiding it at the same time. Consequently, everyone benefits even if initially the parties themselves were reluctant to cooperate, since conflict can bring improvement and growth if dealt with appropriately.

Obviously one of the contributing factors for avoiding dealing with conflicts and not requesting others to do so, as already mentioned, is the lack of skills, common practice, systemic encouragement and support for dealing with conflicts constructively. Hopefully, this book will contribute to a shift towards the situation where dealing constructively with conflicts is more common practice than it is now.

Early Conflict Intervention

Early conflict detection (conflict sensitivity) is a crucial precondition for early conflict intervention and for keeping communication at a high level of quality. As already mentioned, people tend to postpone or avoid dealing with conflicts which only makes the matters worse. So the sooner the better should be a rule of thumb.

There are two obstacles for that however; one is late detection (due to low conflict sensitivity) and the other is lack of clear procedure to deal with the issue. Everything that demands conscious effort or is not clear contributes to it being postponed.

One counter measure for that is making it as clear as possible how a person should respond when sensing a conflict and is not sure how to deal with it. One option in this respect should be talking to the in-house mediator.

As a rule of thumb, if the issue is pressing enough to talk or want to talk about it with someone (but not the one it relates to), unless it is something nice we want to share or something we want to 'brag' about, then obviously, it is something that needs to be dealt with one way or another.

So, if there is an issue that you do not know how to tackle, go talk to the in-house mediator who will either direct you in terms of how to proceed or will assist you in gaining clarity on what the problem is and how to deal with it yourself.

The other counter measure relates to late detection. Namely, the sooner we detect conflict the sooner we will be able to deal with it. But how to detect it sooner? It is about developing conflict sensitivity as described earlier in this chapter, not only in terms of our own conflicts but also in terms of noticing disruption in interaction among others. The more this quality is developed, the sooner we can detect disputes and respond to conflict. Furthermore, raising the standards of quality communication presents a context that contrasts destructive interaction, so the higher the quality of interaction, the sooner we can detect disruptions.

5. Why Wait for Conflict?

If dealing with conflicts constructively is such an important task and if conflicts are inevitable, why would one just wait for them instead of coming to meet them before they even occur? If the sooner we deal with them the better, and the longer we wait, the higher the price we pay, would it not be wise to confront them as soon as possible rather than try to avoid them?

The Price We Pay for Conflict

When conflicts occur and are not resolved or transformed soon, we pay a substantial price, not only in money but also in health (physical and psychological), vitality, motivation, general wellbeing, time, etc.

There are several negative consequences of unresolved conflicts in general like: lack of good atmosphere, lower quality of communication and deteriorating relationships, disintegration of organization or relationship, stagnation, excommunication, violence, abuse and oppression, psychological disorders, psychosomatic diseases, disruption of optimal interaction, among others.

And there are additional ones related to the milieu where conflicts exist, for example, at the workplace: lower work motivation, lack of cooperation, lower productivity, misunderstandings at delegating tasks, higher costs, difficulties in functioning, possible court procedures, ending of work relationships, distrust in co-workers or employees and others.

In general, each unresolved conflict creates an obstacle for communication. In every relationship, there are many differences and incompatibilities that do not on their own represent conflict. However, as soon as interaction develops in an area where that discrepancy is relevant, it presents a difficulty in interaction and functioning and a conflict occurs. If parties successfully resolve or transform conflict, it disappears; on the other hand, if they do not, which means that they or at least one of them is left frustrated, that particular area of interaction is consciously or subconsciously perceived as dangerous or troublesome.

Consequently, parties repeatedly engage in destructive conflict interaction related to that particular area on the one hand and try to avoid or bypass it on the other. Irrespective of their response, either by conflict or by avoiding conflict, productive communication in that area is blocked. Since areas of interaction are also related to each other, the conflict gradually spreads.

As demonstrated in Figure 4 each unresolved conflict presents an obstacle to productive communication in the future until it is resolved. Eventually, such unresolved conflicts pile up and in time make it close to impossible to communicate productively with each other. Consequently, destructive interaction is more and more common and eventually (if nothing changes) the relationship is doomed to end.

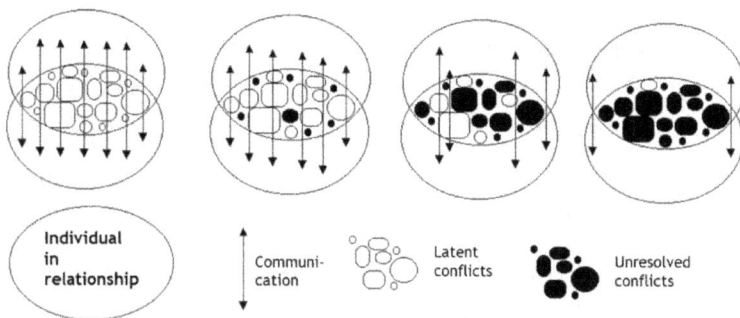

Figure 4: Decrease of possibilities of productive communication between parties as a consequence of unresolved conflicts (Iršič, 2004)

Why People Avoid Conflict?

There are many areas of communication within each relationship and people have several more or less important relationships. In each area within each relationship there is potential for conflict, which is a pitfall in communication that brings us to destructive interaction, which means a state of weakness and self-absorption.

Being in a state of weakness and self-absorption is not pleasant and people tend to avoid unpleasant situations. And people in general tend to view difficulty in conversation as 'a difficult issue' or 'a difficult person' rather than difficulty in interaction.

Consequently, they tend to avoid issues that lead to conflict and individuals who they get involved in conflict with, rather than trying to use appropriate support for fixing the interaction with a specific individual about a specific issue or topic.

Furthermore, there seems to exist an illusion of harmony that is strongly present and resistant to counterevidence. Due to this incorrect presupposition we, as a society and as individuals, tend to neglect development of conflict resolution skills. Consequently, it is also lack of skills that contributes both to a delusion that if there is a conflict, that is the other person's fault, as well as to a tendency to avoid conflicts if possible since they present a situation which we are not trained for nor skilled in dealing with.

Be Faster than Conflict

Avoiding conflicts can be detrimental to the quality of interaction, therefore it is wise to start early and confront them before they grow. But how can we do it if we seem to be half blind in early conflict dynamics. Again, this skill has to be obtained gradually but if we use the mapping approach to communication, described in the previous chapter, we can foresee pitfalls and avoid them, as well as develop skills to transform the 'dangerous zones', so we can transform communication before it becomes conflictual.

Developing Capacity for Personal Strength and Responsiveness

Like in physical fitness, it is also in communication and especially in dealing with conflicts that the capacity of individuals and of groups or organizations as a whole plays a major role. Therefore, individual capacity for preserving internal strength and responsiveness in the face of smaller or bigger differences is crucial. One could also call that transformative capacity of individuals and communities.

Transformative capacity is important because it is often not about the facts, although it seems so and facts are easier to talk about, but about how we are treated as human beings and how safe and strong we feel.

If we have a "bad day", even with the same "facts" we get into conflict more easily and also the impact of conflict is worse than another time when the same facts seem "harmless".

Being aware of these dynamics is in itself empowering since we can "postpone" difficult interaction until later when we feel stronger. And we can also inform others about our state of strength at the given moment and they could, while understanding the dynamics of conflict, agree to deal with "things" another time.

On the other hand, it is important to also be able to "get it together" when needed and to "snap out of it". Being able to do so is empowering on a different level.

In any case, it is important to develop capacity to observe and act according to our inner state of strength or be able to change it and to know what we have to do to achieve that. And it is also important to develop the capacity to listen and be responsive to the other (understand what they are saying, consider their point of view, reflect how we understood them, etc.). This capacity, i.e. to be able to observe, take into account and to change our inner state of strength, as well as to be able to listen and be responsive to others can be called transformative capacity.

Like with sports, martial arts or other skills it must be trained and practiced in order to achieve a higher level of competence and higher levels of quality of interaction within a particular relationship or organization. And the more we practice, the better we become at it.

Consequently, every conflict can be perceived not only as an opportunity for growth but also an opportunity for practicing transformative communication skills and developing transformative capacity.

Developing a Norm of Quality Communication

In addition to enhancing transformative capacity, constructive and high-quality communication should be the norm, especially in cases of conflicts or discrepancies. No conflict should be left to end destructively and if parties need help for that, it should be provided.

At the same time, willingness and effort to sort things out constructively should be requested from all.

Oftentimes people 'drop' issues when they sense tension or conflict and sometimes that even makes sense. However, this tactic is overused and it contributes to people avoiding to talk about things which may lead to tension, or being very careful or even afraid and unsure (lower level of empowerment) when talking to certain people and/or about certain issues. There is obviously no real need to talk about everything if things are not relevant to common goals but nevertheless it is important to be able to talk constructively about anything since one never knows when he/she will accidentally tap into a delicate subject.

Another overused response is when a conflict occurs, people do not talk it through efficiently, but after thinking about it, when they calm down, they realize it was not so bad, or even worse, after calming down (and possibly talking to one or more other people about it), they just push it away or disregard it and continue behaving as if nothing has to be fixed. Again, sometimes this makes sense but much less frequently than it is used. The problem with it is that there is an existing conflict (not only a danger of it), which affects the quality of communication between the parties in general, and a perception of the other distorted by the conflict which was left unresolved.

Therefore, transformative outcome should be requested in such situations and everybody should be aware of that and willing to contribute to it. In terms of the field of spirals, it is important that we do not create holes in the field, or if we do that we mend them sooner rather than later.

So, if high-quality and constructive communication is not a norm, there are many holes in the communication field which present pitfalls for communication in the future.

6. Communication Wellness

Communication wellness can be understood in at least two different ways. The first is communication wellness as a state of affairs in a certain relationship or organization in general, as well as at a specific moment and the second is communication wellness as a service or intervention.

Communication Wellness as a State of Affairs

To understand the concept of communication wellness as a state of affairs we can imagine any relationship and ask ourselves how good the quality of our communication with that person is in general (e.g. from 1 to 10, 10 meaning the best, 1 meaning very bad) and how good it is in a specific moment.

Wellness of our communication varies from person to person and also from moment to moment. Every time we have a fight with a person even if it is a person we get along well with in general, the level of our communication wellness at that moment drops drastically. It normally gets restored relatively quickly (e.g. within an hour or a day) but as a matter of fact it does not need to drop at all.

However, more and more frequent and increasingly intense drops of our communication wellness can seriously undermine our communication wellness with that person in general. Consequently, our relationship is not as good as it used to be.

On the other hand, sometimes after a conflict manifests itself in a certain relationship, parties improve their quality of communication and even relationship, despite the fact that there was a drop in communication wellness. This phenomenon is indicative of the fact that the quality of interaction (e.g. constructive or destructive), including reflection and follow-up communication, determines the outcome more than the immediate emotion of the parties involved.

Similarly, we can assess the level of quality of communication in relation to the whole department or company in general and also in specific situations. Changes of quality of communication at the level of organization are not so rapid as in one-to-one situations but the recovery time is also longer. The impact on communication can persist even when the reasons for that change disappeared. For example, conflict between coworkers can affect the general atmosphere and the impact can still be there even when these coworkers resolved or abandoned their conflict and communicate well again. Even more, the changed atmosphere can feed back the tension between them.

The quality of our communication also affects our perception and attitude towards the other person. Just imagine how benevolent you are to a person during a fight or how benevolent you are towards a person you have a bad relationship with. And also how you perceive the other person in these situations. On the other hand, remember how sometimes only one nice remark changed your perception of the other person for the better. And how differently you interpret actions by a person you get along well with in comparison to actions by someone you dislike.

Communication Wellness Questionnaire and Assessment

As explained above, there are at least three aspects of assessing communication wellness, namely: 1. current quality of interaction with a particular person or within a group 2. general state of affairs with a particular person in terms of quality of communication and 3. general state of affairs in relation to communication within an organization.

The assessment of communication wellness is to a certain extent subjective since it depends on perception of the parties involved (the same situation which someone might perceive as destructive communication may be fully enjoyed or appreciated by the parties) but it is nevertheless helpful to have a tool for assessing it more reliably. With this aim I present the questionnaires below as a help to assess the quality of communication.

For each aspect of the assessment respondents can answer on a scale from 1 to 10 (1 meaning not at all and 10 meaning absolutely).

It is helpful to assess the perception of the quality of interaction even though it is subjective. In fact, it is precisely this subjective perception that counts and affects further interaction the most.

In addition, we can find out if people estimate the quality of communication similarly and how it is or is not similar – so we can then work on improving certain aspects of it if necessary – or if people estimate the quality differently and why – so we can discover the reasons for discrepancy (e.g. differences in assertiveness, etc.) and decide what to do about it.

Quality of communication within an organization or a group in general

For each of the statement below mark (with grades from 1 to 10) to which extent you agree with them, where 10- means I agree completely (the most) and 1 – I do not agree at all (the least).

1. The quality of our communication in general is very high.	1 2 3 4 5 6 7 8 9 10
2. I feel that I am listened to by the others in general and that what I say counts.	1 2 3 4 5 6 7 8 9 10
3. I can express my opinions and concerns without fear of being rejected.	1 2 3 4 5 6 7 8 9 10
4. I feel I can talk to the others about anything that is relevant and seems important to me.	1 2 3 4 5 6 7 8 9 10
5. I can share or discuss a problem that I see or have with the others constructively	1 2 3 4 5 6 7 8 9 10
6. I want to listen to the others and appreciate what they have to say.	1 2 3 4 5 6 7 8 9 10
7. In general, I understand what the others are speaking about.	1 2 3 4 5 6 7 8 9 10
8. I can listen to the others also when they seem to be upset.	1 2 3 4 5 6 7 8 9 10
9. I feel respected and appreciated.	1 2 3 4 5 6 7 8 9 10
10. Conversations in our organization always end constructively.	1 2 3 4 5 6 7 8 9 10

Quality of communication with a person in general

For each of the statement below mark (with grades from 1 to 10) to which extent you agree with them, where 10- means I agree completely (the most) and 1 – I do not agree at all (the least).

1. The quality of communication with the other in general is very high.	1 2 3 4 5 6 7 8 9 10
2. I feel that I am listened to by the other and that what I say counts.	1 2 3 4 5 6 7 8 9 10
3. I can express my opinions and feelings without fear of being rejected	1 2 3 4 5 6 7 8 9 10
4. I feel I can talk to the other person about anything that is relevant and important to me	1 2 3 4 5 6 7 8 9 10
5. I can share or discuss a problem that I see or have with the other person constructively.	1 2 3 4 5 6 7 8 9 10
6. I want to listen to the other person and appreciate what they have to say.	1 2 3 4 5 6 7 8 9 10
7. In general, I understand what the other person is saying.	1 2 3 4 5 6 7 8 9 10
8. I can listen to the other person also when they are being upset.	1 2 3 4 5 6 7 8 9 10
9. I feel respected by the other person.	1 2 3 4 5 6 7 8 9 10
10. Our conversations always end constructively.	1 2 3 4 5 6 7 8 9 10

Current quality of communication with a specific person

For each of the statement below mark (with grades from 1 to 10) to which extent you agree with them, where 10- means I agree completely (the most) and 1 – I do not agree at all (the least).

1. Our communication with the other in this particular moment is constructive.	1 2 3 4 5 6 7 8 9 10
2. I feel heard and understood.	1 2 3 4 5 6 7 8 9 10
3. I can express my opinions and feelings without being rejected.	1 2 3 4 5 6 7 8 9 10
4. Is my contribution in communication appreciated?	1 2 3 4 5 6 7 8 9 10
5. I feel calm, confident and clear.	1 2 3 4 5 6 7 8 9 10
6. I feel confident enough to be able to listen to the other person.	1 2 3 4 5 6 7 8 9 10
7. I understand what the other person is saying.	1 2 3 4 5 6 7 8 9 10
8. I can imagine how the other person feels.	1 2 3 4 5 6 7 8 9 10
9. The other person speaks calmly, and he/she is respectful to me.	1 2 3 4 5 6 7 8 9 10
10. I am happy with the way, how our conversation is unfolding.	1 2 3 4 5 6 7 8 9 10

In addition to explicit and conscious assessment we can briefly check-in (with ourselves or with the other) using only one or all three questions below more intuitively:

1. How good do I feel in this communication (e.g. from 1 to 10)?
2. Do I feel I am listened to and understood?
3. Do I understand what the other person is saying and do I demonstrate that?

It takes just a moment to check-in on that but it can be of significant help in preserving or regaining a high quality of communication.

Communication Wellness as Intervention

Communication wellness as a service or intervention is offered by a trained professional who helps the participants who have otherwise good communication with each other but

1. have specific issues they want to discuss or resolve and want to preserve or raise the level or quality of their communication, or
2. want to improve their communication wellness in general.

Communication among participants is consequently more enriching and productive, as well as less threatening and painful as it could otherwise be.

Communication wellness can be used whenever parties feel or perceive that their communication is not optimal. It can be also used as a support in communication when they want to make sure that communication does not go wrong. In terms of a specific form any of the interventions listed in the next chapter can be used. The key difference is not in the format but rather in the stage when it is used, that is at a stage when there is no conflict. Communication wellness as a service therefore preserves or even enhances communication wellness as a general state of affairs in a particular context.

If people do not have a conflict, that still does not mean that their communication is optimal, therefore even if there is no conflict they can benefit from improved quality of interaction either in a particular area or in a particular relationship in general. However, even when people say they do not have a conflict, it is often the case that they just do not label disruptions in interaction as conflicts, they do not consider them as something abnormal (which is unfortunately the case) or they do not want to make a big deal out of something they can endure. If that is the case, even more so, they could benefit from improved quality of interaction. In both cases, communication wellness might be the appropriate intervention or service for achieving that goal.

Opportunities for Wellness or Proactive Mediation

There is a fine line between communication wellness (service) and proactive mediation since support is similar and relationship is good in both cases. The distinction lies in whether there already is a conflict, misunderstanding or disruption in communication (proactive mediation), or whether we would like to avoid the con-flict, or even if there is no danger of that at all but the parties want to improve their communication or discuss a possibly complex or difficult issue on a higher level of quality (communication wellness).

Listed below are some examples (far from being a complete list) of opportunities for wellness that you can consider. Again, the same situation might be considered proactive mediation, depending on whether the difficulty already exists or is perceived, or not.

1. Topics we avoid
2. Conversations that did not end well despite our good intentions
3. Conversations where we did not feel heard or understood by the other
4. Conversations where we are in doubt whether the other felt heard and understood
5. Topics that we do not know how to bring up

Topics we avoid

Think of a topic that you think would be important to talk about with somebody and which you are avoiding. Why are you avoiding it? Are you worried it could go wrong? Do you not know how to start? Do you not know how the other would respond? Do you not want to hurt or offend them? Was it never the right time?

There are plenty of reasons why people avoid certain topics. Sometimes, it is obviously wise or polite to do so but in most of the cases it is related to not knowing how to do it (skills) or not wanting things to go worse (outcome) or both. Consequently, things which would be better if they were discussed or resolved, remain unspoken but nevertheless hinder the quality of interaction. Obviously, this is not the case if it is a minor or unimportant thing but we usually do not avoid such a topic. We merely forget about it or decide to drop it and do not think about it anymore. So, if the topic reoccurs in our mind, it is obviously important enough to do something about it.

Conversations that did not end well

Think about a conversation that you or the other side started but did not end well in spite of your good intentions. How did it make you feel? Were you angry or upset or hurt or frustrated? What did you do with those feelings? Why did it not end well? Were you too pushy? Were you accusing or attacking the other? Were you defensive? Was it the wrong moment? Was the other side not in the right inner state? Did the other side not want to listen? What did you do about it afterwards? Did you start it another time? Did you just drop it? Did you talk to someone else about it? Did you tell others about how uncooperative the other was?

There is no harm per se if conversations sometimes do not end well. What is important is what happens afterwards. Too often it never gets resolved. Oftentimes we just let it go and even forget about it, but nevertheless the 'emotional sediment' remains and starts to accumulate. With every conversation that does not end well there is less optimism and motivation for talking things through. And it bears real consequences for that relationship and organization. Additionally, many times both parties talk about that to somebody else or even more people and rarely in a manner seeking transformative support but more often complaining or blaming the other and consequently remaining in the state of weakness and self-absorption on the one hand and also spreading bad atmosphere by impacting (even if at a subconscious level) the attitudes of others towards the other party and by that contributing to 'emotional pollution' of the company.

Conversations where we did not feel heard or understood

Think about a conversation when you did not feel heard or understood. It may not have ended badly but still you were frustrated. When we do not feel heard and understood, it adds a bit of frustration. We normally let it go but it nevertheless stays with us. Our confidence in terms of being able to get the others to listen is affected slightly as well. Maybe the conversation did not end badly on the surface, but it left a scar.

And it could very well be that we were wrong or that what we wanted to say did not make sense and we could have discovered that through dialogue if we were heard.

Obviously, it could be that it was not the right time for conversation, that the other was under pressure and unable to listen or that the issue was or seemed to be unimportant (but if that were the case, then the feeling of not being heard would not stay but would disappear).

It may also be that the other did not want to hear or try to understand us for various reasons which may be legitimate in a particular situation (e.g. the other person was working, was under stress, our approach was aggressive, etc.) but all those reasons if communicated in the situation or later would again make the feeling of not being heard disappear, especially if we were able to talk things through at the end.

Obviously, I do not mean to say that one has to be completely heard and understood about every little thing in every situation and that everything else must wait. There should be an appropriate time and place for every conversation. But what I am saying is that if experienced oftentimes, the feeling of not being heard or listened to piles up and affects our attitude and perception. We start being convinced that the other person does not want to hear or understand and we feel rejected in that relationship. It further affects our communication and cooperation with that person and our motivation to contribute altogether.

Conversations where we are in doubt or feel that the other side did not feel heard and understood

On the other hand, sometimes the other side may not have been heard. Maybe we were too focused on what we wanted to say and did not try to listen? Maybe they did not say what they wanted or were not assertive enough? Maybe they even did not know or were unsure what they wanted to say? Regardless of the reason, if the other person did not feel heard, it may have a similar impact as the one described above. One option for dealing with that is to check with them. To explain that we feel that maybe they did not feel heard and ask them how they feel about it and listen to them. On the other hand if we were willing to listen and understand in the first place, that may not have been the reason but something else might have been.

Topics that we do not know how to bring up

Think of a situation when you did not know how to start a conversation or how to tell somebody something important. It is a subset of topics we avoid but we do that for a specific reason, namely not knowing how to bring it up. Consequently, we delay talking about it and it may have negative consequences for us, as well as for the interaction. It could also be that it is because it is not clear to ourselves what we wanted to say or maybe we did not see how talking about it could help or maybe we were not sure how the other would respond and wanted to postpone the frustration. Or it may be for any other reason, but in any case, we and the quality of communication with the other could benefit if this was clear at least to us, that is to say if it becomes more clear to us what we want to talk about, with what goal and whether we want to bring it up and how we want to do it. Transformative conversation could help us with that.

Any other topics

In fact, regardless of where we start the conversation, if it is transformative, it will lead us to important issues or topics that are blocking our optimal interaction and communication with that person, so even if we start with an issue that is not so important, we will eventually discover more relevant issues. The advantage of transformative communication is that it is 'fixing itself' so to speak, which means that when interacting in a transformative manner, regardless of the issue, the quality of communication is improving and if faced with an obstacle, the obstacle itself can become an issue and is dealt with on the way.

Assessing Communication Wellness Policy

Oftentimes, when being asked or thinking about the quality of communication in our organization we rely on subjective assessment or 'feeling' about it. Feelings, although very important, are not objective and they can be influenced by our mood, situation, opinions of other people, etc. So, it is useful to have a checklist or a set of criteria to analyze what we want to assess. We propose below a set of questions that can be compared to the organization's practice and the situation to get an estimate of how established and clear the communication wellness policy is.

Questions for assessing communication wellness policy:

1. Do we have communication standards by which we measure the quality of interaction?
2. How do we detect conflicts in our company?
3. Which indications of conflict do we consider?
4. Do we have a protocol for dealing with conflicts?
5. What are third parties who observe or suspect conflict required to do?
6. What are the parties in conflict required to do?
7. Is it a responsibility of the employees to respond appropriately to a detected conflict?
8. Do we have internal mediation service?
9. How do we know if a conflict is successfully resolved?
10. Are employees well informed of the options and procedures for dealing with their own conflicts or conflicts observed among coworkers?
11. Is constructive conflict resolution encouraged and how?
12. Is resolving conflicts part of the job description of employees?

7. Options for Intervention

When a need for the improvement of communication is detected or there are indications of conflict, there arises a question of how to respond. When in conflict, people are reluctant to talk directly to the other party (for fear of making it worse or the response being destructive, based on a lot of negative experience as to the responsiveness of the other or due to a perception that it is the other person's fault).

Therefore, many times conflicts are suppressed or avoided and not dealt with appropriately. Consequently, the quality of communication and cooperation among persons involved deteriorates. In order to prevent such unwanted outcomes, there needs to be a set of readily available options for intervention that are known to and appreciated by the receiving parties, as well as potential interveners.

In addition, sorting out conflicts and preserving high quality of communication should be a permanent item in the job description or included in the professional responsibility of employees and managers, as well as referring coworkers to manage the conflict when a disruption of communication wellness is noticed.

Possible Interventions and Options for Support

The following pages list and briefly describe some possible interventions and options for support to deal with conflicts.

Mediation

Mediation refers to a deliberate process between parties in conflict or with misunderstanding supported by a trained mediator in order to resolve or overcome conflict between them or to improve the quality of their communication. Parties can request mediation by themselves or can be referred by a third party. Or one party can ask the mediator to invite the other party. In all cases participation in mediation is voluntary.

There are in general two options for mediation: 1. in-house or internal mediation which is conducted by a trained mediator who is also part of the organization or 2. external mediation conducted by an independent mediator hired for this purpose. Obviously external mediation is less readily available, more expensive and more formal but on the other hand the external mediator is not involved in everyday life of the organization, can be a professional mediator and can be perceived as being more neutral.

Mandatory mediation

Mandatory mediation refers to mediation when parties do not necessarily want to participate but the mediation is required by company policy (in certain cases), ordered by a judge, required by contract, demanded by the owner of the company or the manager, etc. Mandatory mediation makes sense especially when third parties suffer consequences of unresolved conflict, e.g. the working atmosphere and the efficiency of the team is affected; children are exposed to tension and misunderstanding of parents; the functioning of a company is inhibited because of the conflict within, etc.

Non-formal mediation

Non-formal mediation refers to conversation supported by a trained mediator within the context of a meeting, a conversation, negotiations, etc. without considering the process as (formal) mediation. The mediator takes part in the conversation but consciously adopts a neutral and supportive role and therefore contributes to a more constructive manner of communication.

Communication wellness

Communication wellness as intervention refers to transformative support of conversation between parties similar to mediation, only that there is no conflict or disagreement between parties. The relationship between parties, as well as quality of communication is high but they still want to benefit from high-quality support in order to make sure that conversation does not go sideways or that it is as productive as possible, or just to let themselves be 'pampered' by a third party and enjoy the process and the outcome of the conversation even more.

Using mediation skills

In addition to non-formal mediation which refers to a situation where the mediator is in the neutral and supportive role for the whole time, using mediation skills only in parts of conversation is also useful. It refers to a situation within another context (e.g. meeting, negotiations, conversation, etc.) where one side intentionally supports part of the conversation in order to make it more productive. It is not a mode of intervention per se but rather enhancement of or support to the quality of communication when needed. Mediation skills can be used by a third party involved or present in the conversation or by one or both/all parties themselves.

'Undercover' mediation

'Undercover' mediation refers to a situation where one or more participants in the situation (e.g. meeting, negotiations, etc.)

intentionally adopt a neutral supportive role in advance in order to support the quality of interaction of the rest and therefore ensure or contribute to positive interaction and productive outcomes. Unlike undercover agents, however, nothing bad happens to mediators in case they are found out since they try to support all parties to achieve the best outcome.

Designated mediator

A designated mediator is a person who is assigned to remain neutral in the conversation and offers transformative support to others. Similarly to a designated driver who remains sober in order to be able to get the others home safely and reduce the risk of a car accident, a designated mediator takes care of 'safety' in communication and contributes to a lower risk of destructive conflict, especially when a conversation is more complex or involves delicate issues. Unlike the undercover mediator, however, where others are not necessarily aware of his or her role, the role of a designated mediator is known in advance and others can count on him or her.

'On the spot' mediation

The term 'on the spot' mediation refers to a situation when a conflict occurs or manifests itself within a certain situation and the parties choose to or are instructed to deal with it on the spot, either within the situation or separately (e.g. in the next room) with the help of a trained mediator, either from within the group or one that is immediately available.

'Communication first aid'

The term 'communication first aid' refers to a response by third parties to a misunderstanding or quarrel of people in their vicinity, either they are friends, family members, co-workers or also strangers who just happen to be near them at the moment. It is somewhat similar to 'On the spot' mediation only to a smaller extent.

Unlike with bodily injuries, where it is expected that bystanders help the injured parties, it is in general true that bystanders in a conflict do not help or they even walk away from the situation or tend to take sides, which normally makes things worse. Contrary to that, one can offer 'communication first aid' to the parties in conflict by supporting their interaction to be more productive. Of course, the intervener has to be skilled in the transformative communication approach in order to be able to help, otherwise they can also make things worse (like someone who would try to help with an injury but has no knowledge how to do it).

The difference between 'on the spot mediation' and 'communication first aid' is that by latter situation is not yet resolved (unless it is a minor matter) and it can continue later on by another intervention or by the parties themselves.

Coaching

Coaching as intervention refers to a conversation of a trained professional with one party in order to support the party in elaborating on the issues, dilemmas, decisions or conflicts, as well as on how to proceed with communication with the other party (co-worker, spouse, boss, etc.). The coach does not give solutions or instructions on how to proceed, but helps the parties to decide and gain skills and confidence to deal with the situation constructively.

Transformative conversation

Similar to coaching, transformative conversation supports the speaking party in elaborating on issues, dilemmas, decisions or conflicts, as well as on how to proceed with communication with the other party. The listener does not have to be a trained professional but does need to have mastered transformative communication skills in order to be able to offer high-quality support to the speaker. Transformative conversation can be used between co-workers, friends, spouses, parents and children, neighbours, etc. when the speaking party has a dilemma, pending a decision, problem or conflict with someone and he/she is not sure how to proceed or became stuck.

Referral to mediation, coaching or transformative conversation

If one does not have the knowledge of how to help, one can still help by calling a mediator or referring parties to mediation either directly (on the spot or later on) or also indirectly (through the mediator or mediation coordinator). When referring to mediation or other support, however, it is important to act in line with the transformative support model, namely that we aim at empowering parties, rather than trying to force them to go. It is also important that each coworker is at least roughly familiar with different modes of intervention (e.g. mediation, coaching, etc.) and their specifics, so he/she can help others consider possible options and choose the most appropriate one for their situation.

Reflection (after the conflict)

Reflection after non-optimal communication with somebody is also very useful. It is more focused on the past, rather than on the present or future communication in order to identify reasons and possible alternatives to our behavior or responses. It is crucial, however, that it is focused on our own behavior and responses in terms of taking responsibility (not blame) for our actions or words or lack thereof. Reflection can be done by someone on their own, but it is more useful if it is supported by a trained third party (either a mediator or a coach) or a competent coworker, since that way it can be more thorough and could also help us see the things which we would otherwise miss. In any case, it is easier and more comfortable with the support of a trained person. Support by someone not competent for the task can be less optimal or even damaging, especially since people are not used to adopting a neutral stance and offering support at the same time, so they might either take our side or defend the other, which would in both cases make it harder for us to transform our perception and attitude.

"Self-mediation"

Self-mediation refers to a situation where one or both/all parties who are trained in mediation or transformative communication skills resolve to employ them consciously in their conversation in order to either resolve an issue or prevent conflict from happening. It is especially useful in good relationships for less difficult conflicts or for conflict prevention.

Obviously, it is much more difficult than mediation (with all the rest, e.g. parties, issue, situation, being the same) since in addition to being focused on the conversation, one has to take into account also the transformative aspect of interaction, which is (even if not simple) much easier for a mediator since s/he is not involved in the discussion. And with the support of a mediator the conversation is much easier for the parties as well, since even if they pay attention to the quality of their interaction, the mediator only contributes to it being even better.

The table above lists the interventions in this chapter according to whether intervention is scheduled separately (e.g. mediation), takes place in the situation (e.g. 'communication first aid') or if it is designed for an individual (e.g. coaching).

Training in transformative communication skills

In order for the employees to be able to use transformative communication skills, a training course of those skills has to be provided, either as in-house training or with an external institution that offers such training courses. Obviously, training courses for small groups or practicing within small groups can be encouraged within the organization. There are two advantages of developing these skills: firstly, employees will be able to sort out issues progressively more and more themselves and secondly, even when using transformative support, they will be more able to participate constructively. In addition, employees will develop transformative capacity in general and will be able to sort out things in their personal lives more easily as well, which will in turn also benefit their wellbeing at workplace.

Separate intervention	Intervention in situation	Individual participation
• Mediation • Mandatory mediation • Non-formal mediation • Communication Wellness	• Using mediation skills • 'Undercover' mediation • Designated mediator • 'On the spot' mediation • 'Communication first aid' • "Self-mediation"	• Coaching • Transformative conversation • Reflection • Referral

Table 6: Options for intervention

How to Intervene

When intervening, it is important to act in line with the transformative support model, namely that we aim at empowering parties when intervening, especially when referring them to mediation or other support. We should make sure that we are in the state of strength and responsiveness before we decide to act. If we act from a state of weakness and/or self-absorption, we are more likely to add to the problem than the other way around.

If we are not sure how to deal with a situation, we can always turn to the mediation coordinator or in-house mediator about this and 'pass the baton' to them or get support in how to deal with the situation ourselves. For example, if there are two colleagues who seem to have an issue or there is something that feels wrong, but we are not sure what it is nor does anyone tell us and we do not want to 'make things worse', we can first consult the in-house mediator ourselves.

On the other hand, if a coworker turns to us and starts explaining a problem he or she has with another coworker or the manager, we are not supposed to immediately go to the mediation coordinator (although that still is an option for later), but we can (if we can spare the time) listen to them and use transformative skills, and maybe that would suffice. But if we notice that listening to them contributes to our state of weakness, either because we agree with them or because we disagree or because we do not have time or energy, then it is better to excuse ourselves and ask them to postpone the conversation for later or suggest that they should talk about it with either the manager or the in-house mediator.

Many times, it is easier to talk to a coworker, but unless he or she is competent to offer appropriate support, people just spend time (although there is some comfort in talking about things to someone) and do not solve the problem. In addition, they use the other person's time (and energy) and contribute to spreading the negative atmosphere in the organization, since they talk about the problem and others do not know what to do with it, on the one hand and on the other hand, they do not want to talk about it to the manager in order not to get the one who told them into trouble. So, the negative energy spreads and can gradually poison the atmosphere in the organization without anyone wanting it or knowing they are contributing to it.

Therefore, it is important that every employee knows how to deal with a situation like that, namely, listen to the person using transformative skills, postpone the conversation or suggest talking to the mediator or if none of that works, talk to the in-house mediator or mediation coordinator themselves.

When to Intervene

It is important to intervene as soon as possible (with appropriate intervention), possibly even before the conflict appears. Definitely, as soon as signs of disruption in communication occur or there is any sign of weakness and/or self-absorption.

The idea is **not to endure as much conflict as possible but to transform it as soon as possible**. That way conflict can even be fun to solve and sorting it out is really like communication wellness and not something difficult. If relationships are good, communication and even differences in opinions are enjoyable, so it would be a waste of energy and damaging to the atmosphere if one were to wait for conflict to escalate before using intervention. By attending to conflicts or even differences early, one has the option to get the most out of them for the least amount of effort, time and cost. The longer one waits the worse the consequences and the harder the solution.

Obviously, that does not mean that people should not be able to communicate and sort things out on their own and that they should go to mediation for every little thing. It does mean, however, that quality communication should be encouraged and supported. If the parties benefit from using the support (they either save time, enjoy more or come to a better solution or just make sure things do not go wrong), it is better they use the support and not sort things out themselves, which would result in a lesser outcome and a higher cost.

In the long run, however, it is exactly by using transformative support that the transformative capacity of individuals (including communication skills) and the general transformative capacity grow, so people are able to sort out increasingly difficult issues by themselves and they even enjoy it.

Which Option for Support to Choose

In general, a rule of thumb should be: use a less formal option first, so sometimes just using skills or communication first aid would suffice, or maybe transformative conversation with one of the parties would resolve the issue. Other times, however, coaching or mediation would be most suited. And other times only obligatory mediation could do the job.

There is no rigid rule as to which intervention is the best. It is important, however, that intervention is suited to the situation. If there is a minor misunderstanding, then referring parties to mediation would appear to be exaggerated. On the other hand, if there are strong signs of weakness and self-absorption, just using the skills for a few minutes would not do the job.

Obviously, the parties should also have a say in the matter. If parties are confident that they will be able to sort it out themselves, for example, they should be given a chance.

On the other hand, if at least one of the parties seems reluctant to talk to the other directly, or if they express (directly or indirectly) that they could use support, then formal or non-formal mediation should be considered.

In any case, it is important to decide on the timeframe and measures of success (unless on the spot mediation is used). For example, until when will the parties deal with the issue, and how will they know that the problem is sorted out.

At the same time, especially if it is not a minor matter, it is important to allocate sufficient time and decide who is going to offer transformative support in advance, otherwise things easily get postponed due to a lack of time but also due to a feeling of uncertainty about dealing with the issue.

Being Alert and Responding Appropriately to Disruptions

An important aspect of intervening timely and appropriately is being sensitive to disruptions in interaction. Not sensitive in terms of being upset and frustrated with every disagreement but being able to recognize conflict, as well as being able to tolerate substantial amount of it, and seeing it as an important task to decrease or transform conflict as much as possible, to improve the quality of interaction.

Like someone who is tidy and can tolerate a substantial amount of disorder, but nevertheless sets to clean up even small things immediately and consequently has less work, the mess does not pile up and he enjoys a higher level of quality of the environment. Even more than cleanliness, the quality of communication affects our general wellbeing, so maintaining a high level of quality and responding promptly to disruptions should be an important task for all involved.

After all, even if it is a conflict that does not concern them, why should people have to be exposed to the presence of conflict between others and suffer a decrease in quality of the atmosphere? Especially, since the existence of conflict which is not dealt with tends to make matters worse.

8. New Communication Standards for Organizations and Society

Being able to read and write and to use the computer are skills that an employee is normally expected to possess. The ability to use the computer is something that one often does not even think about. This is even more true for reading and writing. However, this was not so normal in the past.

On the other hand, conflict competence and conflict resolution skills are not something that is widely thought of or expected, despite the fact that a lack of those skills can seriously hinder work effectiveness and undermine the efficiency of achieving the goals of an organization. One of the reasons for that is also the lack of general awareness regarding conflict and communication.

In light of that, this chapter proposes and describes new communication standards for companies and organizations, as well as illustrates them with examples and suggests options for their implementation.

All employees, management and the owner/s:

- Understand the transformative model of communication and conflict
- Are able and willing to use transformative mediation skills (reflecting, summarizing, checking in) in the face of adversity
- Are able to assess their own wellbeing (strength and responsiveness) and predict or enquire about the same with the other party
- Are able to recognize a situation where parties are stuck in place or spiraling down, for their own conversations, as well as the conversations of colleagues
- Are willing to self-refer or go to mediation (transformative support) if referred by a third party or invited by the other side
- Know how and when to refer others to mediation (if perceived as useful)
- Know the options and how to access transformative intervention, if needed
- Are able to use (at least on a basic level) transformative communication skills in their own disagreements with others
- Are aware of the company's policy regarding communication wellness

As an organization:

- Have a clearly established policy with respect to communication wellness and tools for intervention
- Have several options for intervention available, including internal/in-house mediation and/or external/independent mediation
- Have a suitable number of employees trained as mediators and have external mediators available
- Have all employees trained in offering and accepting referral to mediation
- Have all employees trained in using transformative communication skills
- Have constructive conflict management included in the job description of every employee and manager
- Include a mediation clause in every contract, especially employment contracts

Standards in Relation to Individuals

In terms of standards which relate to every individual, the company can make sure that every employee is trained to meet these standards, or an assessment of that can be integrated in to the selection of employees or the hiring process. Irrespective of the way they are met, it is important that employees are clearly aware of them and know that meeting them is expected.

Understanding the transformative model of communication and conflict

The foundation for improving or maintaining a high level of quality communication is having a tool for assessing its quality and understanding its dynamics, that is having a map or a model for that. The transformative communication model, as briefly described in chapter one, can serve as such a tool.

Although it is possible to understand this model to a certain extent by reading about it, it is better and easier if one can discuss it with someone who already understands it (e.g. in training), especially if it is to have practical relevance for everyday functioning. It takes time and thought to fully grasp this idea and even more so to understand it in everyday context.

Being able and willing to use transformative mediation skills in the face of adversity

Transformative mediation skills (reflecting, summarizing, checking in) are a very useful tool when miscommunication or misunderstandings appear. By consciously using these skills when needed, the likelihood of a conflict drastically decreases. Even if conflict does appear, it is using these skills appropriately that can defuse or even resolve the conflict on the spot. Consequently, all involved can save time and energy and preserve good communication.

In addition to having the skills, one must also be willing to use them, even if it seems easier to just avoid a situation or respond 'spontaneously', which most of the time means responding in a nonproductive or even destructive manner.

For example, if two colleagues, when discussing a certain issue, seem to get stuck or seem to go in circles, just doing a summary might disentangle the situation. Or in another case, just a few reflections might do the job. Whereas if others only wait (and feel frustrated) or go away, the parties may not be able to sort it out so efficiently by themselves and it could add to the negative atmosphere.

Transformative mediation skills are not simple even if they may seem so at first glance, especially due to the fact that people are in general not trained or used to be neutral. Therefore at least some training is necessary to understand and practice these skills.

Recognizing a situation where parties are stuck in place or spiraling down, for one's own conversations, as well as the conversations of colleagues

Recognizing a destructive conflict interaction as early as possible is crucial to preserving the wellness of communication. If we fail to notice the signs, it may be too late to save the situation or it can be much harder to do so.

On the other hand, if people are trained to notice the indications of nonproductive conversation in their interaction or in that of their colleagues, they can intervene sooner, either on the spot or by referring parties to transformative support. Sometimes even a minor intervention can prevent the deterioration of communication.

Being willing to self-refer or go to mediation (transformative support) if referred by a third party or invited by the other side

Deciding to use mediation or accepting an invitation or referral to mediation can be challenging. When one is in conflict, he or she does not necessarily feel like talking to the other about the issue at hand, the more so the stronger the conflict. On the other hand, conflict affects not only those involved, but also their surroundings, therefore it is important to deal with it constructively.

Deciding on mediation requires a relatively high level of inner strength and awareness of the importance of conflict transformation, so a-priori willingness and commitment to use mediation in case of misunderstanding is usefull in this respect.

For example, if we have a conflict with somebody in the company (even if it is not a big problem), we may avoid doing something about it. On the other hand, if we committed to use mediation in advance, and we know that the other side has done the same, it is much easier to propose mediation or accept the invitation.

Again, some training or exercise in this respect is useful, since people are in general not used to proposing mediation and they might refrain from doing so just because they do not know how.

Knowing how and when to refer others to mediation

Many times, it is not clear if one should intervene, propose mediation, help in the conversation or if parties even want this or would perceive this as intrusion. The truth is, however, that people in conflict oftentimes feel left alone with their problem and appreciate concern and offers of support (providing that it is done the right way), even if it is only a question if they need support, or if they considered mediation, or how they are doing. Failure to intervene is also related to not knowing how to intervene. Consequently, many times 'bystanders' do not do anything (or even worse, take sides) when conflict or a decrease in the quality of interaction occurs.

For example, if we see that two colleagues are at odds and we know it would be good for everyone if they sort things out, but are unsure as to how or what to do, we will most likely do nothing.

By being trained and knowing when and how to refer to mediation, the amount of prevented conflicts or conflicts attended to early on will increase, which will benefit all involved.

Knowing the options and how to access transformative intervention if needed

Sometimes people feel the need or are willing to use support in their conflict or situation, but they might not know who or where to turn to or what the appropriate option for their situation is. Even if they are willing to use support, they do not use it since it is not clear enough or it is too complicated to access the appropriate support. Therefore, knowing how to reach for help or who to turn to is important for every employee.

The possibilities for accessing transformative support should be very simple and readily available (e.g. each employee having contact details of the in-house mediator or mediation coordinator with his or her name, telephone number and email address and the encouragement to contact them even if only to consult about a situation).

In addition, being aware of the options and having a list of them with a short description (e.g. in a booklet) is important since simply looking at different options on the list makes it more likely that we will choose one and, irrespective of which one we choose, the process has started and the parties can always choose a more appropriate option later.

Being able to assess one's own wellbeing

Oftentimes people are not aware of their inner state, e.g. frustration, anger, fear etc., or do not pay conscious attention to it. In part because managing one's own inner state or emotions is not a skill widely held or thought of. However, the inner state, especially the level of strength or weakness and the level of responsiveness or self-absorption play a key role in the quality of interaction and consequently in the outcome. For this reason, it is crucial to be able to assess one's own inner state and refrain from engaging in difficult conversations while in a state of weakness and self-absorption.

For example, if we notice we are frustrated because the other party is not listening to us, it is a sure sign of a relative weakness on our side, so we have several options; either to shift focus and listen first (which is in general a good idea), or postpone the conversation, or suggest a break or invite a colleague to 'mediate' the situation. However, if we do not notice our own frustration, it is likely we will act on it and try to force the other to listen.

Even more than understanding the transformative model, learning how to assess one's own inner sense of strength requires practice and cannot be learned theoretically.

Predicting or enquiring about the wellbeing of the other party

Similarly, it is important that the other party is in a state of strength and responsiveness. If they are not, they will not be able to listen in that moment. If we correctly assess their wellbeing at the given moment, we can adapt our approach and listen and empower them first, if they are disempowered, postpone the conversation altogether or suggest mediation, or just bring up the issue, if they are in a state of strength. If we are not sure what their inner state is, it is better to ask then to get it wrong.

For example, if we are not sure about the other's inner state, we can check with them and ask: *How do you feel?* or *Are you comfortable with this conversation?* or *Do you feel ok?* However, if we notice that the other person is very focused on what they think or say or if they show signs of frustration and/or seem to be unable to listen to what we are saying, or they disagree with almost everything we say, it is most likely that they are in a state of self-absorption and, consequently, it does not make sense to try to explain things to them at that time, but rather try to support and empower them first. Oftentimes, listening to our own feelings can give us an insight into how the other side feels. If we feel frustrated, there is a good chance that the other side feels frustrated as well. So, we can either check in with them or observe whether our observation confirms our feelings, and if it appears that we are right, we might adopt appropriate strategies for that.

As for assessing our own internal strength, developing a skill for assessing the inner state of the other also requires some training and practice and cannot be learned merely theoretically.

Being able to use transformative communication skills in one's own disagreements with others

Obviously, it is not practical to end a conversation and go to mediation for every minor disagreement, nor is it useful to just drop the issue when we disagree. Therefore, it is important that employees have the skills to use transformative communication (at least on a basic level) so they can sort out minor disagreements themselves (on the spot or later). Together with assessing one's own wellbeing and checking in about the same with the other, this is a very important quality of employees and managers alike.

As previously suggested, merely a summary or a few reflections might do the job (if a third party does it) and the same is true if one or both of the parties use those skills. Sometimes, for example, an invitation: *Let us both say how we understood each other, to see if we got it right?* can make a huge difference rather than each repeating what they have already said.

As the rest, using the transformative communication skills requires some training and practice. However, the more they are practiced in everyday conversations, the more they become natural. At the beginning, with people not being used to it, they may seem awkward or unnatural, but with increased experience along with witnessing its beneficial effect, they become easier and more natural to use.

Being aware of the company's policy regarding communication wellness

In addition to the qualities described above, it is important that each coworker is aware of and knows the company's policy with respect to communication wellness. Besides the obvious fact that one has to know about something in order to act accordingly, it also means that, by learning about it, coworkers can understand how it should work and have reassurance that they should not suffer and be left alone due to unresolved conflicts or bad relationships. And, furthermore, that there is support provided and that it is the company's intention to keep a high level of quality in communication and that contributing to it is also their responsibility.

Standards in Relation to an Organization as a Whole

In addition to standards which relate to individuals, there are also standards relating to the company or organization as a whole which support and complement the described qualities of employees.

Having a clearly established policy with respect to communication wellness and tools for intervention

A clear policy that is known to all employees should be adopted with respect to achieving and maintaining communication wellness within the organization. It is also important that it is available in writing and accessible to every employee. If the policy is not clearly established, it contributes to unclarity, confusion and reluctance to act in line with it for fear of doing something wrong, especially if it is not common practice. In addition to adopting the policy, it is crucial to clarify it with employees to make sure that it is understood correctly and accepted.

It is also important that it be regularly revised, discussed and refined in accordance with practical experience and its impact on the quality of communication (within the organization, as well as with clients and partners). If it is not consciously considered and modified, if necessary, it can become distant from practice and eventually something without any practical relevance.

Therefore, it has to be the result of collaborative efforts where everyone feels involved and their input is valued. It should be written in clear, every-day language, so that everybody can understand and practice it.

Having several options for intervention available

For employees to be able to refer to, self-refer to or accept invitation to mediation or another mode of support, they obviously must be available. Therefore, the company must provide several options for intervention, including internal/in-house mediation and external/independent mediation.

Ideally, the company should provide or make available all of the options listed in chapter seven, but at least external mediation, in-house mediation, non-formal mediation, transformative conversation and training in transformative communication skills should be provided.

In addition, they should be clearly established in the organization's policy and available (e.g. in a booklet or otherwise) to all employees together with the name, telephone number and email address of the contact person for each of them (e.g. for coaching there may be a different person than for mediation).

Having a suitable number of employees trained as mediators and external mediators available

It is also important to have a suitable number of employees trained as mediators to be able to provide in-house mediation service, but also to make it possible to use non-formal mediation, 'on the spot mediation' and 'communication first aid', among others, and to facilitate the use of transformative communication skills in the organization.

Ideally, the organization should have at least 10% of employees trained in transformative mediation, so they could manage in-house mediation without adding too much to their workload. The presence of trained mediators will by itself have a positive impact on the quality of communication, in terms of using transformative communication skills in everyday situations and it will make it easier to intervene on the spot or facilitate using mediation or other transformative process, if needed.

Obviously, having so many trained mediators is not a small task, so having them trained one by one is a reasonable path to getting there. However, even if it is not possible to achieve the ideal proportion, each employee or manager trained in transformative mediation contributes to mediation and transformative communication skills being more present in everyday functioning of the organization.

In addition to having internal mediators present at the workplace, it is important to have a list of external mediators readily available, either on a case by case basis or by contract. What is important is that they are contacted in advance and they agree to be readily available in case of conflict, so the company can call on them if needed.

The advantages of external mediators are obviously that they are not involved in the everyday functioning of the company and that they can be very experienced, professional mediators, which is especially important for more difficult cases or for the disputes or misunderstandings in management or between the owners of the organization.

Having all employees trained in transformative communication and basic mediation skills

In addition to having trained mediators, the use of transformative communication skills in one's own disagreements and for assisting the others should be promoted. As already discussed, it should not be the case that people go to mediation for every small disagreement, nor should they just let them go. But since disagreements are a fact of life, progressively integrating the use of transformative communication skills into the functioning of the organization is important for achieving and preserving communication wellness.

In addition to using these skills in their own disagreements, employees should be trained to use them with colleagues when they perceive they have issues requiring transformative communication skills. Rather than 'being polite and minding their own business' they should intervene using those skills if interaction becomes destructive. Obviously, this does not mean giving their own opinion on the matter nor moralizing or patronizing the parties in conflict (which would most likely elicit a negative response), but using transformative skills and remaining neutral and consequently helping the parties regain their own constructive mode of interaction.

As already mentioned, the organization can provide training courses for all employees or it can require these skills when hiring an employee (as part of the initial training or as a requirement for getting the position). In any case, it is important that all employees are familiar with these skills and are committed to using them.

Having all employees trained in proposing and accepting referral to mediation

In order for employees to competently refer, accept referral or self-refer to mediation, they have to be trained in those skills. It is not an everyday event that we are referring someone to mediation or that we receive referral to mediation, so it may be awkward to even think about it. Training and rehearsing such procedures can contribute to familiarizing the employees with the processes and increasing the likelihood that they will be used in real situation, when appropriate.

Again, the company can require those skills at the beginning, before hiring an individual, or provide such training as part of employment, either internally or externally. Irrespective of the above, however, it is important to provide periodic training to refresh and improve skills needed for proposing or referring to mediation (which can also be combined with discussing and refining the policy and practicing transformative communication skills) to help sort out any possible dilemmas or difficulties that arise over time.

Including constructive conflict management in the job description for every employee and manager

Including constructive conflict management in the job description contributes to conscious acceptance and promotion of quality communication. It becomes an explicit focus of attention. Although we are aware that relationships and communication are important, we in general invest relatively little conscious attention to this area. Many times, we hear responses like: I have so much work to do, I do not have time to deal with this, referring, obviously, to some kind of interpersonal situation. Deliberately putting the dealing with conflicts constructively into work assignments changes the status on a symbolic level and contributes to it being assigned a higher priority than before.

At first glance, spending time dealing with a conflict seems a waste of time, but in the long run, especially if the process is successful, it represents investment in the quality of cooperation and prevention of negative consequences of unresolved conflict.

Including a mediation clause in every contract, especially employment contracts

Including a mediation clause in a contract has a symbolic, psychological and also legal relevance. On the symbolic level it represents values of amicable conflict resolution and trying to work things out rather than imposing decisions. On the psychological level it prepares parties to search for a solution if a problem occurs and encourages them to use mediation if needed. And in the legal sense, a mediation clause presents an obligation to try sorting things out with mediation first, before deciding on other options, including litigation. It also complements the fact that constructive conflict management is included in the work description of employees and managers.

Gradual Implementation of Communication Wellness

If an organization does not already function in accordance with the standards described above, it is not an easy task to implement them, the more so if the organization is big. It is therefore important to implement them gradually and strategically. If people are used to a certain way of functioning and communication, especially with respect to conflict, they do not change their ways easily. And one can also not impose or command the change, since change happens on different levels. Not only on the behavioral level, but also on the emotional and cognitive levels.

Especially in the process of establishing these standards in an organization, but also later on, it is important to provide training in transformative communication and training in referral to transformative support for all employees.

People have to start seeing conflicts in different ways than before. To see conflicts as an opportunity and not as a problem caused by the other or others and which should not occur in the first place. Additionally, the values of individuals and of the organization as a whole have to change accordingly. It is therefore by no means a simple task but it is worthwhile nevertheless.

A change of any sort, and especially such a change which, to a certain extent, changes and demands the change of the perception of the basic elements of life, may represent a challenge, or even a conflict in itself. So, it has to be dealt with appropriately and in line with a transformative approach. The organization should transform from a conflict-avoiding or conflict-denying to a conflict-resilient organization and to an organization committed to establishing and preserving communication wellness.

Conclusion

Even though I firmly believe that using suggestions and implementing the standards described in this book would contribute to better success of an organization in financial terms as well, at least in the long run, I cannot promise that.

What I do think, however, is that it is worthwhile to develop organizations which function in accordance with the communication wellness standards, even if it does not bring any financial benefit.

At the same time, it seems obvious that the quality of communication at the work place presents a significant factor in job satisfaction, loyalty, productivity, motivation and even the health of everybody involved. Unresolved conflicts are a major cause of stress and stress-related illnesses. So even if indirectly, raising communication wellness to a higher level can benefit the organization.

In addition, changing the communication culture for the better within one organization can have a lateral positive effect on other organizations that are in contact with it and also on families and other personal relationships of the employees. The skills learned and practiced regularly at the workplace are spontaneously used in other situations as well, so the level of tension or stress decreases in other areas of life of the employees and, in turn, conflict tolerance for them and for the organization increases.

Nobody wants to live and work somewhere where there are unresolved conflicts and bad communication, but that is often the case. It is not because we would choose to, but because we – as a society – have not yet learned sufficiently to master interpersonal communication. And also because of the lack of awareness and a systematic approach to raising and preserving the quality of communication. To be fair, however, we should recognize that there are some successful companies, groups or families that consciously and systematically or at least intuitively pursue that goal and are successful in it. While that is not generally the case, by using the suggestions in this book, instituting its suggestions, and obtaining additional competence trough training courses, workshops and practice, we can all learn, grow and develop skill, that can change all of us for the better.

References

Bush, R.A.B. & Folger, J.P. (1994). The Promise of Mediation: Responding to Conflict Through Empowerment and Recognition, Jossey-Bass, San Francisco

Bush, R.A.B. & Folger, J.P. (2005). The Promise of Mediation: The Transformative Approach to Conflict. San Francisco: Jossey-Bass.

Cloke, K. & Goldsmith, J. (1997) Thank God it's Monday! 14 Values We Need to Humanize the Way We Work, Irwin Professional Publishing

Cloke, K. & Goldsmith, J. (2000) Resolving Personal and Organizational Conflict: Stories of Transformation and Forgiveness, Jossey-Bass, San Francisco, California

Cloke, K. & Goldsmith, J. (2005) Resolving Conflicts at Work: Eight Strategies for Everyone on the Job, Jossey-Bass Inc., Publishers, San Francisco

Cloke, K. (2006) The Crossroads of Conflict: A Journey Into the Heart of Dispute Resolution, Janis Publications USA Inc., United States of America

Crawley, J. & Graham, K. (2007) Mediation for Managers: Resolving Conflict and Rebuilding Relationships at Work, Nicholas Brealey Publishing, London

Dana, D. (2001) Conflict Resolution, McGraw-Hill, New York

Doherty, N. & Guyler, M. (2008) The Essential Guide to Workplace Mediation and Conflict Resolution: Rebuilding Working Relationships, Kogan Page Limited, Great Britain, United States of America

Fisher, R. & Brown, S. (1988) Getting Together: Building Relationships As We Negotiate, Penguin Books, United States of America

Fisher, R. & Shapiro, D. (2005) Beyond Reason: Using Emotions as You Negotiate, Viking Penguin, United States of America

Fisher, R., Ury, W. & Patton, B. (1991) Getting to Yes: Negotiating Agreement Without Giving In, Penguin books

Folberg, J. & Taylor, A. (1984) Mediation: A Comprehensive Guide to Resolving Conflicts Without Litigation, Jossey-Bass Inc., Publishers, San Francisco

Folger, J.P. & Bush, R.A.B. (eds.) (2016) Transforming Conflict from the Inside Out: Stories and Reflections from Transformative Practitioners, Institute for the Study of Conflict Transformation, USA

Folger, J.P. & Bush, R.A.B. (2010) Transformative Mediation: Core Practices (pp. 31 – 50) in: Folger, J.P., Bush, R.A.B. & Della Noce, D.J. (eds.) Transformative Mediation: A Sourcebook, 2010, Institute for the Study of Conflict Transformation, USA

GLASL, F. (1999) Confronting Conflict, Hawthorn Press

Gottman, J. M. (1994) What Predicts Divorce? The Relationship Between Marital Processes and Marital Outcomes, Lawrence Erlbaum associates, Inc., Hillsdale, New Jersey

Iršič, M. (2004) The Art of Conflict Management (Umetnost obvladovanja konfliktov), Zavod Rakmo, Ljubljana

Iršič, M. (2007) Introduction to Interpersonal Conflict Resolution, Zavod Rakmo, Ljubljana

Iršič, M. (2010) Mediation (Mediacija), Zavod Rakmo, Ljubljana

Iršič, M. (2010b) Workplace Mediation (Mediacija v podjetjih), Zavod Rakmo, Ljubljana

Iršič, M. (2017) Conflict Competence: Understanding, Assessing and Improving the Ability to Deal with Conflicts, Zavod Rakmo, Ljubljana

ISCT - Institute for the Study of Conflict Transformation (2012) Training Manual for International Training on Transformative Mediation: Ideological Foundations and Practice with Joseph P. Folger

Jordan, T. (2000) Glasl's Nine-Stage Model of Conflict Escalation, (http://www.mediate.com/articles/jordan.cfm)

Lederach, P. J. (2003) The Little Book of Conflict Transformation, Good Books, Pennsylvania

Moore, W. C. (2003) The Mediation Process: Practical Strategies for Resolving Conflict Updated and revised 3rd Edition, Jossey-Bass Inc., San Francisco

Patterson, K., Grenny, J., McMillan, R. & Switzler, A. (2002) Crucial Conversations: Tools for Talking When Stakes are High, McGraw-Hill, New York

Rosenberg, B. M. (2003) Nonviolent Communication: A Language of Life, Puddle dancer press

Schrock-Shenk, C. & Ressler, L. (1999) Making Peace with Conflict: Practical Skills for Conflict Transformation, Herald Press

Stone, D., Patton, B. & Heen, S. (2000) Difficult Conversations: How to Discuss What Matters Most, Penguin Books, United States of America

Strasser, F. & Randolph, P. (2004) Mediation: A New Psychological Insight into Conflict Resolution, Continuum, London

Ury, W. (2000) The Third Side: Why We Fight and How We Can Stop, Penguin Books, United States of America

Weeks, D. (1994) The Eight Essential Steps to Conflict Resolution: Preserving Relationships at Work, at Home and in the Community, Jeremy P. Tarcher/Putnam, New York

Winslade, J. & Monk, G. (2000) Narrative Mediation: A New Approach to Conflict Resolution, Jossey-Bass Inc., Publishers, San Francisco

Wiseman, M. J. (1990) Mediation Therapy: Short-Term Decision Making for Couples and Families in Crisis, Lexington Books, Canada

Zumeta, Z. (2000) Styles of Mediation: Facilitative, Evaluative, and Transformative Mediation, http://www.mediate.com

About the Author

Marko Iršič graduated in educational studies and obtained a Master's degree. He is a coach, mediator and trainer of mediators.

He is the author of two previous books in the Slovenian language entitled **The Art of Conflict Management** (Umetnost obvladovanja konfliktov) and **Mediation** (Mediacija) and a book entitled **Conflict Competence: Understanding, Assessing and Improving the Ability to Deal with Conflicts**.

He founded RAKMO Institute in 2003 and it became a leading organization in transformative mediation in Slovenia. He is also a member of the board of MEDIOS – the Association of Mediation Organizations of Slovenia and president of the European Association for Transformative Mediation, as well as a member of the advisory committee of the World Forum of Mediation Centers.

His professional and voluntary work is dedicated to raising awareness about the importance of constructive conflict resolution, as well as raising the quality of communication in interpersonal relationships in general, and teaching skills and sharing knowledge that would contribute to that.

Through his work and observation as mediator, coach and trainer with individuals, couples, neighbors, coworkers, companies and organizations, as well as with government institutions he gradually developed the model and guidelines presented in this book.

About Rakmo Institute

Rakmo Institute (Zavod Rakmo) was established in 2003 with the purpose of raising awareness about the importance of conflict resolution and spreading the knowledge and the skills of constructive conflict management.

Rakmo Institute is a founding member of MEDIOS – the Association of Mediation Organizations of Slovenia, a founding member of the European Association for Transformative Mediation and an active member of the World Forum of Mediation Centers.

It is at present the leading organization in the field of transformative mediation in Slovenia. Rakmo Institute also organized the 1st International Congress on Transformative Mediation in Ljubljana in 2011, the 2nd International Congress on Transformative Mediation in Ljubljana in 2014 and the 3rd International Congress on Transformative Mediation in Ljubljana in 2018.

Rakmo Institute provides training courses and seminars in transformative mediation, transformative communication, communication wellness, conflict management, anger management, stress management and in other areas of communication and personal relationships.

You can contact Rakmo Institute by writing or calling to:

Rakmo Institute – Zavod Rakmo
Parmova ul. 53, 1000 Ljubljana, Slovenia

www.rakmo.eu or www.rakmo.si/home
info@rakmo.eu or info@rakmo.si

+386 1 436 41 17